Tortillas!

Tortillas!

*Pat Sparks and
Barbara Swanson*

ILLUSTRATIONS BY PHYLLIS MASON

St. Martin's Press ● *New York*

Design by Beth Tondreau Design

Library of Congress Cataloging-in-Publication Data

Sparks, Pat.
    Tortillas! / Pat Sparks, Barbara Swanson.
       p. cm.
    ISBN 0-312-08912-0 (pbk.)
     1. Tortillas.   I. Swanson, Barbara. II. Title.
  TX770.T65S66 1993
  641.8′2—dc20   92-41316
                                                      CIP

First Edition: April 1993

10 9 8 7 6 5 4 3 2 1

With thanks, to our Moms!

How could our Moms have known fifty years ago that we would need this photograph in 1993? But that is how our Moms have been to us—anticipating and meeting the needs of our hearts before we knew them ourselves. They have always been right there behind us, believing for the best in our lives.

Around the table, while growing up, we experienced food for our tummies (including our very first tacos and enchiladas!) and food for festivity, sharing, and laughter. Because of our Moms, we have been blessed with the gift of God in our lives—His faithfulness, compassion, love, joy, and communion with others. We will always remember our Moms, and give thanks!

DOROTHY AMLING BOSCH
1917–
BEATRICE LABAHN AMLING
1919–1990

We love you!
Pat and Barbara

Contents

Introduction

We believe cookbooks are meant to expand knowledge and thinking, introduce new ideas, enhance technique, give insight into cultural and social backgrounds, and, especially, make the reader a better cook. We hope ours does all these things.

We feel that the *tortilla* is the perfect vehicle to expand knowledge and enjoyment in the kitchen and in life. Many of the dishes we have included have deep cultural roots, linking us with the traditions of Spain and Mexico, California, Texas, the American Southwest, and with native Indians, making this more than just a Mexican cookbook. It is a *tortilla* cookbook, drawing from each of those cuisines, all of which use *tortillas* as part of their cookery. You can become familiar with the history and the spirit of the *tortilla* by reading the sidebar notes that accompany each recipe. That same *circle of corn* that has graced the tables of Hispanic countries for centuries is now a popular addition to everyday, and fancy, American cuisine.

Our recipes are meant to inspire as well as instruct. Through them, we urge you to experiment freely with what has become one of the most versatile staples the world has ever known, the *tortilla*. We want you to enter your kitchen with *new eyes*, that is, with the confidence to view every food item—from meats and vegetables to beans, spices, and even fruits—as a potential ingredient for a tortilla meal. With new eyes, you can go beyond the classics to make such kitchen delights as *tortilla apple strudel* or *moo shu burritos*. What fun it is to bring the taste and style of many Hispanic and Indian cultures together with just a simple *tortilla*, along with your imagination, and what is already stocked in your refrigerator and cupboard, no matter how meager it may appear. You can create from what appears to be nothing.

In a short time, a full meal can be prepared that is nutritious, simple, earthy, and frequently inexpensive. You will find that most of our recipes use many of the same simple ingredients because the very nature of the *tortilla* invites simplicity and versatility. We invite you to experience that simplicity with the playful whimsy of creativity and joy that only a *tortilla* can give to its cook, and the cooked-for. Perhaps the best gift of all is the one you'll have when you are finished: that sense of fulfillment and contentment that comes when your creative urge is satisfied, particularly when your family and friends are the happier for it.

How to Use This Cookbook

The Recipes and Their Variations

We encourage you to read each recipe—including its variations—in its entirety before beginning. We have tried to come up with the simplest, most basic recipe as a guideline for the cook to build upon, playfully and creatively, being inspired by the *spirit of the tortilla.*

Preparation Time

This entry gives the time needed to prepare specific ingredients and the entire dish before cooking. Assume that Basics, when listed, are already prepared and waiting in the freezer or refrigerator, or that you have their equivalent on hand.

Cooking Time

This entry gives the final frying, baking, or microwaving time needed to complete the dish for serving.

Total Time

This entry shows the time needed from start to serving. It may include marinating, soaking, and resting time. Normally, Total time would equal Preparation time plus Cooking time.

Using Sauces and Salsas

When a recipe suggests the use of a generic red sauce, green sauce, or salsa, any of the specific recipes listed on pages 26–37 under those general categories can be selected. When a specific sauce is necessary, it is specifically named.

Homemade Versus Store-bought

We encourage you to make all your basic ingredients from scratch—the tortillas themselves, the fillings, beans, salsas, and sauces. You'll find basic recipes for all of these essentials in the book. However, it is up to the cook whether to prepare an ingredient from scratch or whether, for convenience or ease, to select an alternative off the shelf at the grocery store or deli.

Cooking Oil

We have listed vegetable oil in every recipe where oil is indicated, for continuity and kitchen convenience. Of course, the cook can choose the house favorite. Or, try lard! Lard is the classic and there may come a time when you want to experiment with it; it does alter the flavor in a very tasty, classical, and traditional way.

Where to Find a Recipe

Since recipes are not grouped in the typical cookbook format of appetizer through dessert, you may want to consult the index when looking for a particular part of the meal. Starting on page 146, the recipes have been indexed by name, by category or kind of meal, and by ingredients.

The Tortilla

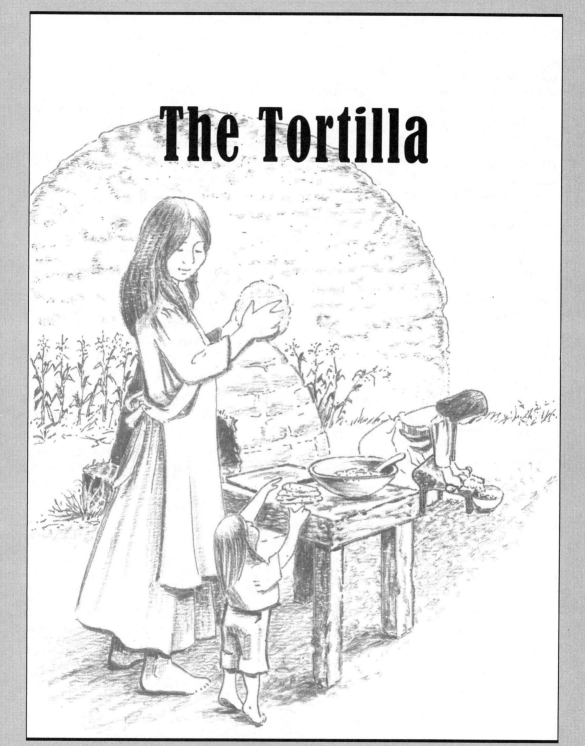

The Spirit of the Tortilla

Just what is the *spirit of the tortilla?*" you ask. At first, we
didn't know the answer either. We also didn't care at first,
but something kept nagging at us to grasp the very nature
of the *tortilla* and understand why it had established itself as
a staple in our families' meals. We started with what we knew.

What we did know was that there was a mystique about
saying "It's tacos tonight!" that always brought a gleam to the
eye and an anticipatory yum to the tummy as the family went
off to school and work. That special *spirit* did not arise when
we said, "It's meatloaf tonight!" It was at work when we said,
"I bought *tortillas* today," yet it didn't work when we said, "I
bought potatoes for the pot roast today." Yet meatloaf and
potatoes were staples, too. What was the difference? We didn't
know. But we sure knew there was a difference.

We also knew that *tortillas* were a significant staple in our
families' meal planning without us ever consciously deciding
they would be: Pat, in Southern California, and Barbara, one
thousand miles north in Portland, Oregon. Why this happened
we didn't know.

What we also knew was that Pat could have three packages
of *tortillas* in the refrigerator, go shopping, see fresh, warm
tortillas being made, and buy them anyway. Fresh *tortillas*
awakened some primal drive. Why? We didn't know.

We knew, too, that the *tortilla* begs the feaster to get involved, to customize his own meal from the items at hand.
Anything goes! *Tortillas* can be rolled, folded, or made into
chips and pieces. They can be left flat and heaped with toppings, used as scoops, edible spoons, or even as disposable
plates that fit an entire meal in the palm of a hand. Only the
limits of imagination stop the inventing. Why this happened
we didn't know.

We also knew that the most favorite *tortilla* meals of all were
the ones at which food was picked up and eaten with the
hands, especially when everyone helped himself from com-
munity bowls, sharing basic ingredients, yet creating his own
taste treat. Why this happened we didn't know.

What we also knew was that *tortillas* seemed to bring out the best among family members and friends gathered to eat. A glow of festivity, earthiness, and togetherness would be present.

Eventually, we realized that during all those years we had been experiencing the *spirit of the tortilla!* Somehow, when those kernels of corn are transformed into a single flat circle, something unique is birthed that is far more than just food.

We invite you to discover the *spirit of the tortilla*. When shared with others, the *tortilla* opens new doors to friendship, eating techniques, and playful ways of preparation. Try dipping into shared bowls of ingredients to heap goodies on top of a *tortilla* for a meal. Look around the table to see how others are building their *tortillas*. Laugh. Point. Hug. One person puts cheese on the bottom; the other puts it on top just because that's the way he likes it. Sharing. Your own thing. Have both. Have fun.

Indeed, somehow, that single circle of corn, the *tortilla*, always carries within it a simplicity that bonds everyone at the table in a warm communion. It is with that very *tortilla* spirit of simplicity, joy, and love that we share our recipes and inspiration with you.

The Origins of the Tortilla

Tortillas haven't changed much since the days of Díaz del Castillo and Calderón de la Barca (see sidebars left and right). Today, whether they are served earthy and plain from the humblest dirt-floored home or with gourmet fillings in an upscale restaurant, *tortillas* are really nothing more than unleavened bread formed into basic, round, thin pancakes. They are the national bread of Mexico and the basis of many dishes.

The *tortilla* was a traditional food among the Indian tribes of Mexico long before the Spaniards began their conquest of the country. It was a food born of necessity for the native Indians, who had to preserve their corn harvest from one season to the next. They learned to dry the corn kernels. Then, as they needed food to eat, the dried kernels were prepared by simmering them in water with lime until soft (*nixtamal*), then laboriously ground by hand on a stone mortar (*metate*). The moistened, fresh, smooth dough (*masa*) was shaped into

"*Tortillas*, which are the common food of the people, and which are merely maize cakes mixed with a little lime, and of the form and size of what we call scones. I find them rather good when hot and fresh-baked but insipid by themselves. They have been in use all through this country since the earliest ages of its history, without any changes in the manner of baking them, excepting that for the noble Mexicans in former days, they used to be kneaded with various medicinal plants, supposed to render them more wholesome. They are considered particularly palatable with chile, to endure which, in the quantities it is eaten here, it seems to me necessary to have a throat lined with tin."
—FRANCES CALDERÓN DE LA BARCA
Life in Mexico, 1838

3

small balls with dampened palms, then patted into a thin pancake and cooked on a lime-treated clay or metal griddle (*comal*). This traditional way of making "bread" can still be observed in old Mexican marketplaces, as described at left in Sunset's *Mexican Cookbook*.

Flour *tortillas* were imported from Mexico's northern state of Sonora by the early Spanish settlers, and this form of *tortilla* eventually migrated to the American Southwest. Flour *tortillas* had the advantage of being a quickbread that could be cooked over a campfire griddle and stretched to hold an entire dinner—in a disposable plate. Flour *tortillas* eventually began to supplement corn *tortillas* in and around Santa Fe, even among the Pueblo Indians.

Flour *tortillas* are extremely versatile and easy to make. They can be made with ordinary all-purpose flour and a rolling pin, and rolled thick or thin depending on the cook's desire. They are so much better than store-bought ones!

Today, increasing in popularity is the particularly nutritious whole-wheat *tortilla*. It is especially tasty when filled with vegetables. Blue-corn *tortillas*, which actually look bluish-charcoal gray, are becoming the in thing in some trendy circles. The Pueblo Indians, who raised many varieties of corn, first introduced Southwest cooks to these interesting coarse and gritty *tortillas*. It has even been reported that chocolate *tortillas* are now being made in Santa Fe. What will be next!

Even though you may be cooking with a *tortilla* that is stamped out by a machine, you can still ponder its origin. You can picture the love pouring into the *masa* with hands forming the dough into *tortillas*. You can even begin dreaming of making your own. On the outside chance that you would want to re-create an old Mexican kitchen in your home some Saturday morning, recipes for making *tortillas* begin on page 8.

How to Buy a Tortilla

Fresh tortillas are becoming easier to find, but quality varies and really good ones are rare. Corn tortillas are usually about 6 inches in diameter; flour tortillas can range from 6 to 12 inches or even 18 inches for a *burrito grande* and such. Our standard for most recipes in this cookbook is 9 inches.

In the Southwest, you will find an assortment of both flour and corn tortillas at room temperature on the grocer's shelf, or you may want to seek out a local *tortillería*. Elsewhere, in supermarkets or health food stores, look for refrigerated or frozen brands. Canned and pre-formed crisped taco shells are a desperate last resort and not recommended.

A corn tortilla should be:

- soft and flexible, not stiff, dry, or cracked
- thin, but not too thin
- whitish, not deep yellow or dark
- finely grained, mealy, not coarse
- corn-tasty, not blah
- fragrant in aroma, not sour

How to Heat a Tortilla

When serving tortillas, you will want them soft, tender, moist, and flexible. To keep them at their best, warm them by choosing one of the freshening and softening techniques described below.

Crisp-fried tortillas are fried whole for the base of a tostada or cut into wedges before frying and used as chips with dips, salads, or casseroles. If frying in oil is not desirable, use the microwave or oven methods for crisping.

Frozen tortillas should be defrosted by opening the package and leaving it at room temperature until the tortillas can be separated easily. Allow about 30 minutes before using one of the softening methods. If tortillas seem a little hard or cracked, dip your hand in water and rub tortillas lightly.

After warming tortillas, immediately place them in a tightly covered dish or a sealed foil packet. Hold in a 200°F oven until all tortillas are warmed. Do not allow them to dry out once they have been heated. For picnics or occasions where tortillas must be held for several hours, wrap them in an airtight foil package and place them in an insulated bag or place them in a cloth and several layers of newspaper.

Steamer. Layer two or three tortillas at a time in a steamer basket or vegetable steamer placed over boiling or simmering water. Cover pan and heat for a few seconds until soft and flexible. If left too long, they will fall apart.

Oven. Wrap stacked tortillas in foil and place in a 350°F oven until hot, about 15 minutes.

Microwave. Wrap a stack of tortillas lightly in paper towels and warm on high for 6 or 7 seconds per tortilla.

Ungreased skillet or griddle. Place tortillas, one at a time, on an ungreased heavy skillet or griddle over medium-high heat. Turn frequently until soft, about 30 seconds.

Barbecue grill. Place tortillas on grill above medium-hot coals until soft, turning once, about 30 seconds.

Oiled skillet. Heat vegetable oil, shortening, or lard in a skillet over medium heat. Place tortillas, one at a time, in oil and turn immediately to coat with oil until soft. Do not allow to become crisp. Drain on paper towels.

CRISPING TECHNIQUES:

Fry. Heat ½ inch vegetable oil, shortening, or lard in a skillet over medium-high heat. Fry whole tortillas or tortilla wedges, turning once, until crisp and golden (about 1 minute). Drain on paper towels.

Barbecue grill. Place tortillas on grill above medium-hot coals until blistered and crisp, turning once. This takes about 1 minute, depending on heat of coals, distance from the coals, and desired crispness.

Oven or toaster oven. Bake tortillas on oven rack in a 450°F oven until crisp.

Microwave. Place tortillas between paper towels and heat on high for 1 to 2 minutes. Check after 1 minute and turn.

How to Serve a Tortilla

Traditionally in Mexico, tortillas are served in a special woven basket made for this purpose and covered with a cloth or napkin. A tightly covered dish or insulated bowl will do, or wrap them in a napkin and place them on a warming tray.

At the table, serve tortillas with butter and tear them into pieces to eat, or spread with butter before serving and present them folded or rolled to keep melted butter inside. It is also acceptable and encouraged to use tortillas as eating tools by folding, wrapping, rolling, or scooping to capture right down to the last succulent juices whatever is on the dinner plate.

How to Store a Tortilla

Any leftover tortillas should be sealed in a plastic bag or wrapped airtight in foil and kept in the refrigerator or freezer. They will keep for several months in the freezer and up to a week in the refrigerator. After reading this cookbook, they won't last that long.

How to Make a Tortilla

Tortillas do take time to prepare and are best made at the last minute. Although they can be prepared several hours in advance and reheated with hardly any change in taste and texture, it is best to serve them fresh and hot out of the skillet.

We will assume your kitchen has no special devices such as a processor or tortilla press, and that if you plan to experiment with this project you would want to do it in as unhurried a manner as possible, reproducing the ancestral method. Actually, we suggest that your dinner guests be invited early to participate in the process, all a part of the dining experience. Laughter will abound. And you may feel more relaxed if you have packaged ones on hand, just in case. . . .

If the following directions seem laboriously long, remember that tortilla making is an art. It is both simple and difficult for someone who has never seen it done. Rest easy: Huntley Dent's *The Feast of Santa Fe* takes six pages, and Jacqueline Higuera McMahan's *The Salsa Book* takes seven pages to explain how it is done, just perfectly! According to both of them, their thorough directions take the place of the masterly grandmother, words attempting to replace the experience of watching.

> "You must try making tortillas on a day when you feel unhurried and you can work to get the feel of the dough, rolling it a little, stretching it, and most important, being unafraid of it. So it is just as well you don't have an aunt who is famous for her light-as-a-handkerchief tortillas breathing down your neck."
> —JACQUELINE HIGUERA McMAHAN
> *California Rancho Cooking*

> "A tender and perfectly made tortilla is a puffed one."
> —HUNTLEY DENT
> *The Feast of Santa Fe*

> "Violin-shaped ones still taste good!"
> —JACQUELINE HIGUERA McMAHAN
> *California Rancho Cooking*

"El que canta, su mal espanto. He who sings frightens away his ill fortune. And on the ranch, eating was a way of singing."
—JACQUELINE HIGUERA McMAHAN
California Rancho Cooking

In *Mexico's Feasts of Life*, Patricia Quintana describes how her grandmother showed her the difference between a city tortilla (one made of purchased dough) and a country one: "On that memorable occasion, Mamanena took a heavy enamel pot filled with water, added the kernels of corn, sprinkled in a little powdered limestone dissolved in water, and set the pot over the fire. After it had boiled for about twenty minutes, she took out one kernel to see if the hull had loosened. Then she took the pot off the fire and let it stand for some hours, an eternity to me, before rinsing the corn until its 'teeth' were sparkling white. Next we hulled the kernels in the Indian way, that is, rubbing them together between our hands. What an unforgettable sound it made, the ancient music of the pre-Hispanic hearthside. And she said

(cont. on next page)

Basic Flour Tortilla

PREPARATION TIME: *10 minutes*
COOKING TIME: *30 minutes*
TOTAL TIME: *90 minutes*

½	teaspoon salt
½ to ¾	cup warm water (be sure it is just warm; hot water makes a tough tortilla)
2	tablespoons shortening
2	cups all-purpose flour

1. Dissolve salt in warm water. Set aside.
2. Cut shortening into flour, using two forks or a pastry blender, until mealy.
3. Drizzle warm water slowly into flour mixture, tossing it with a fork to distribute it evenly.
4. Push dough together to form a soft yet stiff ball. If dough does not form a ball, add water by the teaspoonful, until the stray pieces cooperate.
5. Dust dough ball lightly with flour and knead for about 1 minute. Dough will be smooth and flecked with air bubbles.
6. Rest dough for 30 minutes, uncovered. It is thought that the longer it rests (a siesta?), the greater the elasticity of the dough. The process matures it.
7. Pinch off 12 pieces of dough and form into balls. Rotate ball in one hand as you smooth out the edges underneath with the other hand.
8. Place each ball of dough on a board. Use the heel of your hand to flatten each ball into a 4-inch circle. Allow dough to rest for another 30 minutes. Or you could refrigerate it for up to 24 hours. However, before you roll out the tortillas, be sure the dough is at room temperature (allow at least 30 minutes).
9. Dust each 4-inch circle with flour by dipping it into a small bowl of flour, dredging it well on both sides. Then flatten it on a wooden board.
10. Roll out each circle of dough 7 inches or larger, with a rolling pin, working with quick, short, even strokes.

Roll from the center to the edge of the circle, making a turn of the tortilla after two or three short strokes to keep tortilla round.

11. Stretch tortilla by hand. In Sonora, cooks stretch and pat the dough or flip it Italian style as if making a pizza crust. Be playful! Your yield will be higher if your tortillas are thinner and smaller in dimension. Suit yourself.

12. Cook each tortilla in a 10 to 12-inch hot, ungreased iron skillet, turning it after about 1 minute. After you turn it the first time, it will puff in places and have light brown spots. Turn it only once, dividing the time equally between both sides, for a total cooking time of no more than 2 minutes. Don't push on it where it is puffing; it is forming layers. That's the whole idea! Don't cook them too long because they will get dry.

13. Stack tortillas as they are cooked inside a folded dish towel and put in a plastic bag. Close bag so tortillas will continue to steam and soften. Serve immediately.

14. If made ahead, cool and wrap tortillas in an airtight plastic bag, then refrigerate or freeze.

YIELD: *12 tortillas*

VARIATION: Substitute whole wheat flour for all-purpose flour, or use half whole wheat and half all-purpose flour.

to me, 'Now, we will grind them.' Then she placed the wet kernels upon the metate, picked up the mano, or grinding stone, and began to rub the kernels against the curved stone surface they rested upon, as though she were stretching out a sheet of dough with a rolling pin, using a rhythm and constant backwards and forwards movement. When the kernels were ground to paste, she sprinkled water on them and invited me, finally, to work the corn dough, whose consistency was a brand new experience for me."

Basic Corn Tortilla

PREPARATION TIME: *10 minutes*
COOKING TIME: *30 minutes*
TOTAL TIME: *90 minutes*

Purchase one package of *masa* (raw dough). Dough is highly perishable and needs to be used within a week (check date on the package). The dough is ready to be shaped into those precious walnut-size pieces, to be rolled very thin, or pressed between sheets of waxed paper or plastic wrap (or, if you are really ready for this project, in your tortilla press).

If you really want to go basic for fun, you can try working with *masa harina*. It is widely distributed in the United States and especially produced by Quaker for making tortillas. It is ground parched corn treated with lime. When water is added to this flour, you have fresh *masa* dough.

USING FRESH MASA:

1. Shape dough into balls about 1½ inches in diameter.
2. Place one ball at a time between two sheets of plastic wrap or two heavy-gauge freezer bags.
3. Flatten ball with your hand, then run a rolling pin over it three or four times. Turn tortilla and repeat three or more times until a 6-inch circle is formed.
4. Peel off top layer of plastic wrap and, if desired, cut out a perfectly round tortilla with an improvised cutter (a saucepan lid is perfect).
5. Heat a skillet or griddle to medium-high and lower tortilla onto it. After 30 seconds, flip it over with a spatula or fingertips, if you can take the heat.
6. Bake on second side for 30 seconds.
7. Flip again and tortilla should hiss and puff and be done.

USING *MASA HARINA*:

1¼ cups cold water (approximately)
2 cups Quaker *masa harina*

"Count C——a has promised to send me tomorrow a box of mosquitoes' eggs, of which tortillas are made, which are considered a great delicacy."
—FRANCES CALDERÓN
  DE LA BARCA
  Life in Mexico, 1838

"With a metate, the primitive Indian-stone grain-grinder which was the most important of the culinary equipment, and a pair of strong wrists, you can get to work.

2 quarts well-
  prepared nixtamal
1 metate and mano
1 pair stout wrists
  patience and
  perseverance

"Place one cup nixtamal at a time on the metate. Sprinkle with water to keep it moist, and then with the mano, which is the small hand-stone, in rhythm rub back and forth, back and forth, over and over the moist kernels until they have been reduced to a medium-fine dough which cleaves together. This is masa. Now you have solved the secret of the foundation of the native corn tortilla or the corn covering of the tamale."
—ANA BEGUÉ DE
  PACKMAN
  Early California Hospitality

1. Add water all at once to flour and mix quickly and lightly.
2. Rest dough, covered, for 20 minutes.
3. Make a tortilla as described in steps 3 and 4 above. If tortilla is rather thick with a grainy edge, work a little more water into dough.
4. Continue with steps 5 through 7 as described above.

YIELD: *1 pound* masa *or 2 cups* masa harina *makes approximately 1 dozen tortillas.*

"A quiet tortilla is finished."
—AN OLD SAYING

According to Huntley Dent in his book, *The Feast of Santa Fe*, the Pueblo Indians make flour tortillas fresh for each meal. The women never measure their ingredients; they just have a feel for their dough. The tortillas are used more like a roll to sop up food and sauces than as a holder of food.

"On to California came the tortilla. It changed with the colonial period from the corn masa to the smoothly crushed wheat flour dough. In Mexico the abundance of water made the cultivation of corn easy, while in California the colonists depended on the spring rains for extensive moisture, thus making it easier to broadcast wheat and gather the yield in due time. The California tortilla made from wheat flour became traditional as such."
—ANA BEGUÉ DE
   PACKMAN
   Early California Hospitality

Nutritional Value of a 6-inch Corn Tortilla

Weight:	30 grams
Calories:	65
Protein:	2 grams
Fat:	1 gram (0.1 gram saturated, 0.3 gram monounsaturated, 0.6 gram polyunsaturated)
Carbohydrate:	13 grams
Vitamin A:	80 international units
Potassium:	43 milligrams
Calcium:	42 milligrams
Sodium:	1 milligram
Iron:	0.6 milligram
Cholesterol:	0

—U.S. DEPARTMENT OF AGRICULTURE
Nutritive Value of Foods

Tortilla Basics

The beauty of the tortilla is that it can be filled, sauced, and salsa'd with practically anything to become a delicious, satisfying meal. Once you've discovered the versatility of this wonderful circle of flour or corn, you'll want to keep what we call the *tortilla pantry*, a supply of those simple, basic ingredients that can be transformed in minutes into an exciting meal. From your tortilla pantry, and out of your kitchen, will come a variety of culinary treats. Try anything from Shredded Chicken or Shredded Beef to perfect Refried Beans that can be blended with any of a number of sauces, like a basic Red or Green Chile Sauce. Then, to complete your dish, add a Picante or Tomatillo Salsa, or a quick salsa made from fresh tomatoes in a blender. You haven't really lived the ease and versatility of the tortilla until you have cooked from Tortilla Basics!

The Tortilla Pantry

TORTILLAS!
- flour
- corn

MEATS
- chicken
- hamburger
- beef
- pork

FRESH PRODUCTS
- lettuce
- tomato
- onion
- cilantro
- avocado
- garlic

- cheese: Cheddar and Jack
- sour cream
- eggs

HERBS AND SPICES
- chili powder
- powdered red chile
- garlic powder
- ground cumin
- dried oregano

IN THE CUPBOARD
- enchilada sauce
- taco sauce
- salsa
- tomato sauce
- refried beans
- chicken broth
- green chiles

Basic Tortilla Fillings

The variety of basic tortilla fillings gives power to the cook through versatility, and romance to the mouth of the cooked for. Here is an opportunity for the cook to enjoy cooking some of the classic tortilla dishes and to economize on time by setting the dish aside in the refrigerator or freezer for use days later when you want to dazzle your family's taste buds. The same tortilla basic can be used in two or three totally different recipes, creating totally different taste treats. When your freezer has ready-made, ready-to-go samples of Shredded Chicken, Shredded Beef, Shredded Pork, Ground Beef, and Refried Beans, there's no end to your kitchen's potential. Back to the basics!

Shredded Chicken

PREPARATION TIME: *5 minutes*
COOKING TIME: *20 to 25 minutes*
TOTAL TIME: *40 minutes*

1 medium (3-pound) chicken, cut up or quartered, or 2 medium (1 pound each) whole chicken breasts, halved, or 8 to 10 thighs
Salt
Onion powder
Celery seed
1 teaspoon freshly chopped or dried parsley
¼ medium onion, sliced
½ medium bell pepper, sliced (optional)
4 lemon slices (optional)

1. Lightly sprinkle chicken with salt, onion powder, celery seed, and parsley.
2. Arrange chicken in a single layer in an ovenproof pan.
3. Place onion, pepper, and lemon slices on chicken pieces.
4. Cover and heat in a 350°F oven until done, about 20 minutes.
5. Cool in juices if time permits, peel away skin, remove meat from bone, and shred by hand.

YIELD: *3 cups*

VARIATIONS:

Microwave: Prepare as above, cover with plastic wrap, and microwave on high until done, 15 to 20 minutes. Cool and shred.

Poached: Season chicken, place onion, pepper, and lemon plus 2 bay leaves in a saucepan with 3 cups water and bring to a boil. Add chicken and simmer gently, partially covered for 20 to 25 minutes for whole chicken and 15 to 20 minutes for breasts and thighs. Cool in broth and shred.

Crockpot: Season chicken, place in Crockpot with onion, peppers, and lemon, and add 2 bay leaves and 1 cup chicken broth or water. Cover and cook on low (200°F) for 7 to 8 hours. Cool in broth and shred.

Turkey: A half turkey breast (about 2½ pounds) can be prepared using these same methods. Increase cooking times.

NOTE: For tortilla fillings, use as is or heat with enough sauce or salsa to moisten.

SUGGESTED USES: Enchiladas, Cobb and topopo salads, crocked tortillas, chilaquiles.

Shredded Beef

PREPARATION TIME: *15 minutes*
COOKING TIME: *1½ to 2 hours*
TOTAL TIME: *2 to 2½ hours*

The original name for
this dish is *ropas viejas*
(old rags). Shredding in
1- to 2-inch pieces is
often called *machaca* in
the Southwest.

Mexican cooks
everywhere boil and
shred beef for their
meals, but in northern
Mexico it is done
especially often and the
beef is highly seasoned.

3	pounds lean, boneless chuck roast (could use brisket or flank steak)
1	large onion, coarsely chopped
2	garlic cloves, minced, or ¼ teaspoon garlic powder
2	teaspoons ground cumin
½	teaspoon salt (or to taste)
¼	teaspoon pepper
2½	cups water
⅓	cup red wine vinegar

1. Trim fat from beef.
2. Rub beef thoroughly with onion, garlic, cumin, salt, and pepper.
3. Place in a covered roasting pan with water and vinegar.
4. Bake 1½ to 2 hours at 325°F, or until beef is tender enough to fall apart.
5. Cool meat in broth if there is time. De-fat broth either by straining it or cooling it in refrigerator.
6. Shred and cut meat into 1- to 2-inch-long shreds, clawing at it with a fork or your fingers until it is finely shredded.

YIELD: *6 cups*

VARIATIONS:

Spices: Add to the existing spices or replace the garlic and/or cumin with hot green chiles (4 to 6 jalapeños), stemmed, seeded, and finely chopped. Also add 1 teaspoon oregano and 2 bay leaves

Cooking broth: ¼ cup concentrated lemon or lime juice instead of the red wine vinegar

Cooking: The meat could be stewed in a Crockpot all day!

TIP: Shredded beef can be prepared up to a week ahead and held in the refrigerator, or it can be frozen in 2-cup quantities.

SUGGESTED USES: Shredded Beef Enchilada, other enchiladas, chimichangas, flautas, with scrambled eggs.

> "Tortillas, to the founders of a new country, became to this nation the staff of life. From indian customs were gathered those foods adaptable to the conquistadores' taste. All through the ancient Mexican empire was offered the tortilla which the Spaniards accepted in place of continental bread. Thus, the tortilla became a part of the daily fare, and is found today wherever Latinamerican menus are served."
> —ANA BEGUÉ DE PACKMAN
> *Early California Hospitality*

Shredded Pork

PREPARATION TIME: *2 minutes*
COOKING TIME: *1½ hours*
TOTAL TIME: *2 hours*

2	pounds boneless lean pork
1	teaspoon salt
½	teaspoon dried oregano
½	teaspoon ground cumin
4	peppercorns
1	bay leaf
2	garlic cloves
1	medium onion

1. Place pork in a deep pan and just barely cover with water.
2. Add remaining ingredients.
3. Bring to a boil over medium-high heat. Reduce heat, cover, and simmer gently until just fork-tender, 1 to 1½ hours.
4. Remove pan from heat and let pork cool in broth.
5. Lift meat from broth and shred by using two forks, or place chunks in a food processor with plastic blade and process for about 10 seconds.

YIELD: *4 cups*

VARIATIONS:

Crockpot: Sprinkle meat with 1 teaspoon garlic powder, ½ teaspoon oregano, and ½ teaspoon cumin. Place in Crockpot and pour 1 cup purchased or homemade green chile sauce (pages 30–32) over top. Cook on low setting (200°F) for 8 to 10 hours.

Carnitas: Place cooked pork in a roaster pan and bake uncovered in a 450°F oven until brown and sizzling, about 20 minutes. Remove and shred.

SUGGESTED USES: Chimichangas, tacos, burritos, soft tacos.

Ground Beef

PREPARATION TIME: *5 minutes*
COOKING TIME: *15 minutes*
TOTAL TIME: *20 minutes*

1   pound lean ground beef
1   medium onion, chopped
1   garlic clove, minced
1   teaspoon chili powder
½   teaspoon dried oregano leaves
¼   teaspoon ground cumin
1   teaspoon vinegar
¼   teaspoon salt
¼   teaspoon pepper
1   8-ounce can tomato sauce

1. Brown meat in a large skillet over medium-high heat.
2. Drain excess fat.
3. Add onion and garlic and cook until they are tender and transparent.
4. Add remaining ingredients and simmer uncovered until thickened, about 10 minutes.

YIELD: *2 cups*

VARIATIONS:

Substitute 1 teaspoon ground red chile for chili powder.

Substitute 1 medium tomato, chopped, or 1 cup canned tomatoes for tomato sauce.

Substitute 1 teaspoon Worcestershire sauce for vinegar.

SUGGESTED USES: Tacos, chilaquiles, taco salad.

"Strange to see how a good dinner and feasting reconciles everybody."
—SAMUEL PEPYS
The Diary of Samuel Pepys

"Before 1492, Mexican cuisine had no dishes with beef, pork or lamb. There were no dairy products—no milk, no cream, no butter, no cheese. Fried foods were unknown. After Columbus and his 17 ships and 1,200 men, that all changed: in came horses, dogs, pigs, cattle, chicken, sheep, goats, and the wherewithal to grow onions, grapes, fruit, radishes, sugar cane, lettuce and so on!"
—RAYMOND SOKOLOV
"How to Eat Like an Aztec," from *Natural History* magazine

According to Jacqueline Higuera McMahan in *California Rancho Cooking,* on some of the larger ranchos granted to Spanish settlers, there would be five or six tortilla makers available for large fiestas. It would disgrace the ranchero to run out of tortillas.

Refried Beans

(FRIJOLES REFRITOS)

PREPARATION TIME: *10 minutes*
COOKING TIME: *2½ hours*
TOTAL TIME: *3½ hours*

1	pound (2½ cups) dried pinto beans
6	cups water or broth
2	medium onions, diced
2	garlic cloves, minced
1	bay leaf
¼	teaspoon ground cumin
1	tablespoon powdered chile
¾	cup bacon drippings, butter, or lard (or any combination thereof)
1	teaspoon salt
½	teaspoon pepper

1. Wash beans, place in a large pot, and add water to cover by 2 inches.
2. Bring to a boil over medium-high heat. Reduce heat to low and simmer, uncovered, for 3 minutes.
3. Remove pot from heat, cover, and soak beans for 1 to 3 hours.
4. Return pot to heat and simmer, covered, for 1 hour, stirring occasionally and adding water if necessary to cover beans.
5. Drain and rinse beans, return them to the pot, and add 6 cups water or broth, half the onion, half the garlic, the bay leaf, cumin, and chile.
6. Bring to a boil over medium-high heat. Cover, leaving lid slightly ajar, reduce heat, and simmer slowly until beans are very soft and tender, about 1½ hours. Stir beans occasionally and add water if necessary to keep beans covered.
7. Heat bacon drippings in a large, heavy skillet over medium heat. Add remaining onion and garlic and sauté until tender and transparent.

8. Remove bay leaf.
9. Purée 3 cups of the beans with ¾ cup liquid in a blender or food processor.
10. Add purée to skillet and cook, stirring frequently, until beans are a thick paste.
11. Drain remaining beans, mash coarsely, and add to skillet to warm.
12. Add salt and pepper.

YIELD: *5 to 6 cups*

VARIATIONS:

Optional ingredients to be added with other seasonings: 1 fresh jalapeño pepper, minced; ¼ cup chopped canned green chiles; 1 sprig epazote; ¼ teaspoon ground cloves.

Optional ingredients to be stirred in just before serving: 2 tablespoons chopped cilantro; ½ cup (2 ounces) shredded Jack cheese; ½ cup cream.

Additional ingredients: 1 8-ounce can tomato sauce to skillet before refrying beans.

For Mexican beans (not refried), add a ham hock, ham bone, or ¼ pound cooked salt pork or diced bacon with fat to bean pot along with seasonings. Eliminate puréeing and refrying steps. Beans should be cooked for less time and should be firmer than for refried.

As a side dish, garnish with cheese, sour cream, green onions, or fresh cilantro sprigs.

Substitute black or pink beans for pintos.

SUGGESTED USES: Burritos, bean dip, nachos.

A Mexican meal is seldom complete without the ever-present bowl of beans. They go with everything and can be enhanced with almost anything—herbs, cream cheese, sour cream, chorizo, green peppers, and chiles. From a simple appetizer with chips as a side dish to a main dish of tostadas or burritos, the humble bean is delicious and versatile. This staple in the diet appears most often in the form of rich, thick, refried beans.

Basic Tortilla Sauces and Salsas

Mexican and Southwestern sauces add not only flavor to dishes, but also substance, and, in enchiladas, the sauce is the very essence. Flavors tend to be powerful, robust, and earthy but not necessarily fiery, although you can adjust the degree of hotness from very mild to hot, hotter, and hottest.

RED CHILE SAUCES

The thought of transforming earthy, dried red chile pods into a velvety sensuous sauce can be intimidating unless you have stood at the side of someone who has been doing it for a lifetime, such as an old Mexican *mamacita*. But with a little practice and experimentation, you'll soon develop a feel for the chiles and their consistency, and will become a master at a sauce you can claim as your own. The result will surpass anything you've been served in a restaurant or have poured out of a can. We encourage you to give it a try when you next get a creative-cooking urge.

When preparing a red chile sauce, it's important to use whole, dried chiles. Commercial chili powder is no substitute for pure ground chiles because it contains other spices such as garlic, salt, cumin, and oregano. By using whole red chiles, your sauce will acquire a unique texture and flavor, and it will be similar to the sturdy, everyday sauces of Mexico—made of a thickened solution of powdered chiles and water—that have a musty taste and an almost mystical ability to combine with tortillas, meat, and cheese. Two basic dishes combining all these tastes are Classic Red Enchiladas (page 44) and Stacked Red Enchiladas (page 54).

You should also be aware that your red chile sauce may not turn out the same way each time you make it. This is because chiles vary in taste depending on where and in what season they're grown. In Mexico and the Southwest, every region has its own red chile sauce and it is known by many names (chili powder sauce, red enchilada sauce, salsa de chile rojo, salsa de chile pasilla, and so on). All use basically the same ingredients, but the differences in preparation as well as in soil and climate make for a variety of flavors.

GREEN CHILE SAUCES

Green chile sauce takes many forms, depending on regional cooking methods and regional ingredients. Our own interpretation is as a versatile basic sauce made from fresh, long green chiles and commonly used over enchiladas, burritos, and chiles rellenos. Typically, green chile sauce is very hot, but the heat intensity varies with the type of chile, where it is grown, and the time of the year.

SALSAS

The word *salsa* means sauce in Spanish, but is commonly used to mean the table sauces traditionally presented as condiments. Fresh ripe, raw tomatoes, chiles, onions, and garlic are the basic ingredients. Versatile salsas have now become popular as dips served with corn chips and as ingredients in many main-dish recipes.

Typically, three sauces are presented at the table, and they vary in hotness, spiciness, and texture. Each is used to warmly punctuate any tortilla fiesta. From raw, bold, crunchy, and relishlike to smooth purée, these offerings allow the diner to customize and be directly involved in the meal.

Red Chile Sauce
(FROM DRIED CHILES)

PREPARATION TIME: *20 minutes*
COOKING TIME: *10 minutes*
TOTAL TIME: *2½ hours to overnight*

8   dried red chiles (California, Anaheim, New Mexico, pasilla, ancho, or any combination thereof)
4   cups boiling water to soak chiles
2   garlic cloves
¼   cup vegetable oil
¼   cup flour
    Salt to taste
½   teaspoon dried oregano leaves
¼   teaspoon ground cumin
2   tablespoons vinegar

1. Rinse chiles under cold running water.
2. Pour boiling water into a bowl, add chiles, and soak for several hours or overnight, using a weighted cover to hold chiles under water.
3. Remove chiles, saving the water.
4. Remove stems, veins, and seeds from chiles.
5. Blend a quarter of the garlic and chiles at a time with ¼ cup of the soaking liquid in a blender or food processor until all chiles are puréed.
6. Force purée through a strainer.
7. Heat oil in a medium saucepan over medium heat. Stir in flour and cook until golden.
8. Add chile purée, salt, oregano, cumin, and vinegar to 1 cup of the water chiles soaked in and add to flour.
9. Simmer, stirring frequently, until sauce coats the spoon, adding chile water to thin, if necessary.

YIELD: *3 to 4 cups*

"Chiquito pero picoso. Little but hot (meaning someone small can have much power)."
—MEXICAN-AMERICAN PROVERB

The term *Chile Colorado* often applies to this red sauce.

The large, dark red, smooth-skinned, dried red chiles that are known as either California, Anaheim, or New Mexico, are basically the same. They come from the same vine and are fairly mild, but the ones from New Mexico can be slightly hotter because of the difference in climate and soil. The *pasilla* is dark red and gently hot with a rich, woodsy flavor. The anchos are dried *poblanos*.

Traditionally, tortillas were torn into pieces, fried briefly, and cooked for a short time in a chile sauce. Then they were garnished lavishly.

VARIATIONS:

Milder flavor: Add 1 8-ounce can tomato sauce.

Roast chiles gently before soaking for added flavor.

SUGGESTED USES: Huevos rancheros, enchiladas (stacked or rolled), tacos, tostadas, for moistening in fillings, or as a sauce for meatballs.

Red Chile Sauce

(FROM POWDERED CHILE)

PREPARATION TIME: *5 minutes*
COOKING TIME: *15 minutes*
TOTAL TIME: *20 minutes*

2	tablespoons vegetable oil
2	tablespoons flour
½	cup powdered red chile
2	cups beef bouillon
¾	teaspoon salt
1	teaspoon garlic powder
¼	teaspoon dried oregano
¼	teaspoon ground cumin

1. Heat oil in a medium saucepan over medium heat. Add flour, stir, and cook until slightly brown.
2. Add powdered chile and bouillon slowly, stirring constantly.
3. Add salt, garlic powder, oregano, and cumin.
4. Reduce heat and simmer, stirring frequently, to develop flavors and until thick enough to coat a spoon heavily, about 10 minutes.

YIELD: *3 cups*

VARIATIONS:
Substitute water for beef bouillon.
Add 1 6-ounce can tomato sauce to the flour mixture.

SUGGESTED USES: Huevos rancheros, enchiladas (stacked or rolled), tacos, tostadas.

"Debate rages over whether or not tomatoes are used in cooking sauces such as red chile sauce for enchiladas. Despite the recipes in numerous cookbooks (none of whose authors live in New Mexico), traditional cooked red and green chile sauces do not contain tomatoes. Uncooked salsas, however, usually do."
—DAVE DEWITT AND NANCY GERLACH
Just North of the Border

George C. Booth, in his book, *The Food & Drink of Mexico*, records this sixteenth-century story about a Spanish explorer's first encounter with Indian cuisine:
"What's that?" José pointed to the large brown seeds.
"Frijol," she replied and ladled him a portion.
"What's this red stuff?" he asked suspiciously.
"Tomatl y chile."
He sniffed, and the aroma was heavenly so he took a bite and found the taste even better.
"Bueno," he reported. "The sainted Lord intended my little bacon and onion to live in peace with beans and tomatoes and chile."

Quick Red Chile Sauce

PREPARATION TIME: *2 minutes*
COOKING TIME: *3 minutes*
TOTAL TIME: *5 minutes*

1 10-ounce can enchilada sauce
1 6-ounce can tomato paste
2 tablespoons powdered red chile
¼ teaspoon ground cumin
¼ teaspoon dried oregano
¼ teaspoon garlic powder

1. Combine all ingredients in a small saucepan.
2. Bring to a boil.
3. Reduce heat and simmer slowly for 2 to 3 minutes.

YIELD: *2 cups*

SUGGESTED USES: Huevos rancheros, enchiladas, tacos, tostadas.

"In colonial America, chiles were grown by Thomas Jefferson, who imported seeds from Mexico and planted them at Monticello in Virginia."
—DAVE DEWITT AND NANCY GERLACH
Just North of the Border

From a casual survey conducted by two staff members of *The Oregonian* newspaper, almost 60 varieties of salsas, fresh and bottled, were discovered at a Portland, Oregon, grocery store, not even a specialty shop. They said, "C'mon Baby, light our fire. We easily found 10 or so pepper sauces where Tabasco not long ago was the lone entry. It's a rare market that doesn't have at least three kinds of fresh chilies, plus a few dried." Portland's over 1,000 miles north of The Border!
—*The Oregonian Foodday* August 11, 1992

Green Chile Sauce
(CHILE VERDE)

PREPARATION TIME: *40 minutes*
COOKING TIME: *30 minutes*
TOTAL TIME: *1 hour, 10 minutes*

12 to 15	fresh green chiles (New Mexican or poblano)
2	tablespoons vegetable oil
½	medium onion, chopped
2	garlic cloves, chopped
3	tablespoons flour
2¼	cups chicken broth
1½	teaspoons ground cumin
½	teaspoon dried oregano
½	teaspoon salt
½	teaspoon pepper
1 or 2	fresh or canned jalapeño peppers, chopped, if desired, for extra hotness

1. Roast fresh chiles by placing them on a broiler pan and broiling about 4 inches from heat until completely blistered and charred, turning frequently with tongs.
2. Place roasted chiles in a plastic bag to sweat and cool for 15 minutes.
3. Wearing gloves, remove chiles from bag and remove and discard stem, skins, veins, and seeds.
4. Chop chiles coarsely and set aside.
5. Meanwhile, heat oil in a 2-quart saucepan over medium heat and sauté onion and garlic until tender and transparent.
6. Stir in flour and cook until flour turns slightly golden, about 2 minutes.
7. Remove pan from heat and gradually pour in broth, stirring constantly.
8. Add all remaining ingredients.

9. Heat to boiling, cover, and simmer over low heat for 30 minutes, stirring occasionally. Sauce should be thick enough to coat a spoon.

YIELD: *3 cups*

VARIATIONS:

Pork: Add ¼ to ½ pound lean pork cut into ¼-inch cubes to the sauce with the broth and chiles. Cut pork into ½-inch pieces for a main dish served with flour tortillas to scoop.

Tomato: Add 1 cup chopped fresh or canned tomatoes with the broth and chiles.

Cream: Add ½ cup heavy cream or sour cream to sauce after it has finished cooking.

Tomatillos: Add 1 pound fresh tomatillos or 2 13-ounce cans, drained. If fresh, remove husks, wash, and parboil for 10 minutes. Drain. Purée in a blender or food processor and add with chiles.

SUGGESTED USES: Enchiladas, burritos, chimichangas.

Quick Green Chile Sauce

PREPARATION TIME: *2 minutes*
COOKING TIME: *3 minutes*
TOTAL TIME: *5 minutes*

1   7-ounce can whole green chiles, drained
1   10-ounce can green enchilada sauce
½   teaspoon garlic powder
¼   teaspoon dried oregano
¼   teaspoon ground cumin
1   tablespoon dehydrated minced onion
1   fresh or canned jalapeño pepper, minced

1. Purée all ingredients in a blender or food processor.
2. Place purée in a small saucepan and bring to a boil.
3. Reduce heat and simmer for 2 to 3 minutes.

YIELD: *1½ to 2 cups*

SUGGESTED USES: Enchiladas, burritos, chimichangas, with shredded pork, as a table salsa.

As her contribution to the party, "Mama Chipo walked into the yard followed by her two sons who carried a washtub of salsa pura between them."
—JOHN STEINBECK
Tortilla Flat

"According to the documents of ancient herbalists, capsicum has been prescribed for a long list of maladies from toothaches, sore throats, yellow fever, spring fever, and for languid people who need something to make the fire of life burn more brightly."
—JACQUELINE HIGUERA McMAHAN
The Salsa Book

"There are all sorts of chili peppers, ranging from the kind that scorch your throat a little to the kind that burst into white flame like an atomic bomb as they go down. The hottest you can buy is the *chili jalapeño*—chili of Jalapa. Mexicans eat it raw, and claim that it's good for digestion. God help you if you try to do the same without a long tactical training period in Mexican cookery."
—GREEN PEYTON
San Antonio, City in the Sun

Salsa Picante

PREPARATION TIME: *10 minutes*
COOKING TIME: *0 minutes*
TOTAL TIME: *10 minutes*

2   medium tomatoes, seeded and diced
¼   medium onion, diced
2   green onions, finely chopped
2   fresh or canned jalapeño peppers, finely chopped
2   teaspoons fresh lemon juice
¼   teaspoon ground cumin
¼   teaspoon dried oregano
½   teaspoon garlic powder
½   teaspoon salt
¼   cup fresh chopped cilantro
½   cup canned crushed tomatoes in purée

1. Combine all ingredients except crushed tomatoes.
2. Blend crushed tomatoes in a blender or food processor with metal blade for 30 seconds so that texture is chunky.
3. Add crushed tomatoes to the combined mixture and mix well.

YIELD: *2½ cups*

VARIATION: Substitute 4 to 5 Italian plum tomatoes for less juice and a more acid taste.

SUGGESTED USES: Dips, donkey tails, picadillo, tacos, nachos.

"On all these dishes a good Mexican spreads *salsa piquante* with a liberal hand. It is simply a hot sauce (and I mean *hot* sauce) made of chopped chili peppers and other fiery condiments floating in water or vinegar."
—GREEN PEYTON
San Antonio, City in the Sun

The classic method of making fresh salsa is to use a stone mortar and pestle called a *molcajete*.

Chile should be used first in moderation. You can always add more. Like salt and other strong flavorings, it is impossible to remove.

Jacqueline Higuera McMahan, in *The Salsa Book*, reported that shortly after being brought back from the New World by Christopher Columbus, chiles were recognized by botanists and physicians for their medicinal value. It was advised in one old herbal book to "take a dose of chiles instead of whiskey for the blues; we found no better antidote for bad days than curling up with a good bowl of salsa. Salsa is cheering, low in fats and calories, high in fiber. . . ."

Salsa Fresca

(FRESH TOMATO/GREEN CHILE SALSA)

With salsa fresca, cooks are free to improvise as to method and ingredients. Use whatever ingredients are fresh and in season. Be creative!

PREPARATION TIME:	*10 minutes*
COOKING TIME:	*0 minutes*
TOTAL TIME:	*1 hour, 10 minutes*

4	medium tomatoes, chopped
1	small onion, chopped
1	garlic clove, minced
1	jalapeño chile, seeded and chopped
1	tablespoon lime juice or wine vinegar
½	teaspoon salt
1	tablespoon olive oil

Combine all ingredients and ripen at room temperature for 1 hour.

YIELD: *3 cups*

VARIATIONS:

Additional ingredients: 2 fresh New Mexico chiles, roasted, peeled, and chopped; jalapeño peppers or other hot peppers, chopped, according to taste and tolerance; 3 tomatillos, finely chopped; ¼ cup chopped green onions; ½ avocado, peeled and chopped; ¼ cup chopped fresh cilantro; 1 tablespoon powdered red chile; ½ teaspoon dried oregano; ¼ teaspoon ground cumin; ½ teaspoon garlic powder; ¼ cup ice water, to be added just before serving.

Fresh ingredient substitutes: Use canned Italian plum tomatoes or canned tomatoes with chiles plus one chopped fresh tomato, no matter how green or sorry looking, for texture; 1 7-ounce can chopped green chiles; 2 pickled jalapeño peppers plus 2 tablespoons juice from jar or can, eliminating lime juice or vinegar.

Salsa Fresca is the basic table sauce of all Mexico. It is a simple blend of fresh tomato, green chile, and onion. Made fresh daily, it is found on the table in practically every home and restaurant. It is spooned into and dolloped onto almost any food that appears on the table. Textures range from a coarse relish to runny or puréed.

Any of the following names are used interchangeably for Mexico's basic table sauce: salsa fresca, salsa cruda, salsa Azteca, salsa picante, or salsa Mexicana.

On the ranchos in old California, fresh salsa was referred to as *sarsa*.

TIPS: When chopping by hand, start with the smallest ingredients, working up to the tomatoes, cutting through all the ingredients in one pile. If too runny, add 1 to 2 tablespoons tomato purée. Fresh salsa keeps well for the day but loses fresh taste after that. Simmer briefly to remove a little of the rawness if storing. Salsa will tend to get more *picante* (hot) as it ripens.

SUGGESTED USES: Dip, quesadillas, cheese crisps, tacos.

When food is hot from the fire, it is referred to as *caliente* in Spanish, while spicy-hot is called *picante.*

"Very little chile is used in Mérida [Yucatán of Mexico] cooking, so food here does not have the fiery hot character Mexican cuisine is famed for. Instead, the *chile habanero,* an innocent looking local pepper, usually is served as a condiment on a separate plate. It may be whole, chopped, or blended with tomatoes in a sauce, but however it appears, it is hot."
—A. R. WILLIAMS
"A Different Mexican Cuisine," from *Américas* magazine

Salsa in a Blender

PREPARATION TIME: *10 minutes*
COOKING TIME: *0 minutes*
TOTAL TIME: *10 minutes*

2   medium tomatoes, cut into chunks
½   small onion, cut into chunks
1   garlic clove
1   7-ounce can diced green chiles
2   teaspoons lemon juice or vinegar
¼   teaspoon ground cumin
¼   teaspoon dried oregano
¼   teaspoon salt

Combine all ingredients in a blender or food processor until
puréed.

YIELD: *2 cups*

VARIATION: Substitute 1 14½-ounce can stewed tomatoes for
fresh tomatoes.

NOTE: This salsa keeps well in the refrigerator for several
days.

SUGGESTED USES: Dip, Mexican pizzas, tacos, taco salads.

Tomatillo Salsa

PREPARATION TIME: *10 minutes*
COOKING TIME: *0 minutes*
TOTAL TIME: *1 hour, 10 minutes*

1   pound (10 to 12) tomatillos
½   medium onion, finely chopped
¼   cup coarsely chopped fresh cilantro
2   fresh jalapeño peppers, seeded and minced
1   garlic clove, minced
¼   teaspoon garlic powder
1   tablespoon lime juice
1   teaspoon olive oil
½   teaspoon salt

1. Remove tomatillos' brown papery husks, wash, and finely chop.
2. Combine tomatillos with remaining ingredients, cover, and refrigerate for at least 1 hour to blend flavors.

YIELD: *2 cups*

VARIATION: For a sauce to be used in cooking, eliminate the cilantro, double all other ingredients, and add 1 cup chicken broth. Sauté onions, peppers, and garlic in oil, add remaining ingredients, bring to a boil, reduce heat, and simmer, uncovered, for 25 minutes.

NOTE: Ingredients can be roughly chopped and combined in a blender or food processor. Turn off and on until ingredients are finely chopped, not puréed.

CILANTRO TIP: Dried cilantro in a jar, even the best brand, can best be forgotten—it's just tasteless. For storage, buy a fresh bunch in the supermarket. Wash and dry thoroughly, then freeze the leaves. When frozen, chop them up fine. Keep in a plastic container up front in your freezer. Works perfectly!

SUGGESTED USES: Crab tostadas, tacos, quesadillas, chicken enchiladas.

"It is an amusing scene to witness, [the Indians] collected in large parties with their children seated on the ground, enjoying their frugal meals of tortilios and chile."
—W. BULLOCK
Six Months Residence and Travels in Mexico (1825)

Tomatillos are about the size of walnuts and look like small light green tomatoes with paperlike husks. They have a tangy lemony flavor. Used primarily in green sauces, tomatillos are easy to grow and often reseed themselves and become invasive. Susan Sides once said, in *Mother Earth News*, "They're as prolific as hamsters so be sure to take a good-sized basket when you harvest."

"How do you spell relief? *Capsaicin.* The active ingredient in chiles desensitizes nasal nerves that cause congestion and sneezing. But doctors at Johns Hopkins Asthma and Allergy Center say the *capsaicin* must go directly into the nose to work best. They're experimenting with a nasal spray."
—*The Oregonian Foodday* August 11, 1992

Green Taco Sauce

PREPARATION TIME: *10 minutes*
COOKING TIME: *25 minutes*
TOTAL TIME: *35 minutes*

4   fresh New Mexico green chiles, seeded
2   fresh jalapeño peppers, seeded
1   garlic clove
1   small onion, quartered
¼   cup water
¼   cup vinegar
1   teaspoon salt
1½ teaspoons sugar
¼   teaspoon dried oregano
⅛   teaspoon ground cinnamon
    Pinch of ground cloves
¼   teaspoon garlic powder

1. Grind chiles, peppers, garlic, and onion in a food grinder or food processor.
2. Place in a saucepan, add remaining ingredients, and bring to a boil over medium heat.
3. Reduce heat, cover, and simmer 25 minutes, stirring occasionally until reduced.

YIELD: *2 cups*

SUGGESTED USES: Turkey roll-ups, toritos, quesadillas, tostadas, tacos, dip.

"The principal produce of this hacienda is *pimiento*, the capsicum. There is the *pimiento dulce* and the *pimiento picante*, the sweet fruit of the common capsicum, and the fruit of the bird pepper capsicum. The Spaniards gave to all these peppers the name of *chile*, which they borrowed from the Indian word *quauhchilli*, and which, to the native Mexicans, is as necessary an ingredient of food as salt."
—BERNAL DÍAZ DEL CASTILLO
The Discovery and Conquest of Mexico, 1517–1521

Salsa is naturally low in fats and calories and high in fiber.

Basic to pre-Hispanic condiments are "various algae and pond scum, such as *cuculito del agua*, gathered in baskets and mixed with the herb *epazote*, dried chiles, and salt; the resultant 'dough' (*masa*) is then spread over a corn leaf, steamed like a tamale, and eaten by itself or in stews." They can be bought from fish tamale vendors in Xochimilco and Texcoco.
—RAYMOND SOKOLOV
"Before the Conquest," from *Natural History* magazine

Guacamole

PREPARATION TIME: *10 minutes*
COOKING TIME: *0 minutes*
TOTAL TIME: *10 minutes*

2   large ripe avocados, pitted and peeled
¼   small onion, finely minced
½   small tomato, minced
2   tablespoons salsa (pages 33–37), or 1 fresh or canned
     jalapeño pepper, seeded and minced
¼   teaspoon salt

1. Cut avocados into chunks or slices and roughly mash
   with a fork.
2. Stir in remaining ingredients.
3. Transfer to a serving bowl and serve immediately.

YIELD: *2 cups*

VARIATIONS:

Additional ingredients:

¼ to ½   cup sour cream
1 to 2   tablespoons mayonnaise
     2   tablespoons finely chopped fresh cilantro
     1   tomatillo, minced (this markedly
          changes the taste)

NOTE: Those who are indifferent to avocados often become
avid fans after encountering guacamole. It can be served as a
dip, on salad greens, and as a garnish dolloped over anything
from tostadas to burritos. It is also a mandatory topping for
flautas (page 56) and taquitos (page 63).

TIP: If guacamole is not served immediately, it will turn
brown and look unappetizing. To prevent this, place plastic
wrap directly on the surface of the guacamole.

SUGGESTED USES: Taquitos, flautas, tostadas, tacos.

"Guacamole is prepared differently in various regions of Mexico. In the city of Monterrey, it is garnished to reflect the colors of the Mexican flag: red, white and green."
—PATRICIA QUINTANA
  "A Taste of Mexico," from *Americana* magazine

In earlier times, guacamole was sometimes called Indian butter or poor man's butter.

The avocado tree is a member of the laurel family, and its leaves are used as flavoring in Mexican cooking.

"The word *guacamole* comes from the Nahuatl [Aztec] words *ahuacatl* (avocado) and *mole* (a mixture, or concoction). In Mexico it is often eaten at the beginning of the meal with warm tortillas—and that is how one really savors it."
—DIANA KENNEDY
  The Cuisines of Mexico

Rolled Tortillas: Enchiladas, Flautas, and More

The word "enchilada" means *filled with chile*, or *chillied up*, and is used to describe a rolled tortilla that is both filled with and drenched with pure, red chile sauce.

The simple enchilada arouses a certain amount of passion about how it should be prepared, usually depending upon where you grew up. The first enchiladas were probably made by the Indians in southern Mexico with corn tortillas, and were most likely meatless. The ones that appeared in northern Mexico were made with flour from the wheat introduced there by the Spaniards. Today, there are endless permutations on the chile sauce and the stuffing, and you will find enchiladas filled with everything from lobster to pickled pork to spiced chicken to olives and sharp cheeses. There are even opposing views as to how to roll the tortilla, or whether to roll it at all. That is why you may find enchiladas that are folded or left flat or layered and stacked like pancakes, or even made up as a casserole with bits and pieces of tortillas. The point is that, no matter what the shape, for an enchilada the *chile* is the thing—the main ingredient that gives the dish its name.

There are ten enchilada recipes to choose from in this chapter. Chicken Picadillo is unique in that it uses almonds, cinnamon, and cloves; try it to see how great it is. Lunch sacks or picnics cry out for a change from the sandwich; substituting a Picnic Roll-Up will be a hit. Donkey Tails, a new look for the hot dog, will always bring a grin from your kids. You have never eaten apple strudel until you have made one out of a flour tortilla. Truly, rolled tortillas are awaiting your inventive hand to bring out their best taste.

NOTE: Bake enchiladas just long enough to heat them through, to blend the flavors, and to melt the cheese. If you don't have much sauce left to coat the rolled enchiladas, rub some water on the ends of the rolls to prevent them from drying out. Enchiladas are an easy meal to prepare in quantity and to freeze for reheating in the oven or microwave. They are best, however, fresh from the oven.

Classic Green Enchiladas

PREPARATION TIME: *10 minutes*
COOKING TIME: *10 minutes*
TOTAL TIME: *20 minutes*

¼ cup vegetable oil
1 large onion, finely chopped
12 corn tortillas
4 cups (1 pound) shredded Jack cheese
1 7-ounce can diced green chiles, drained
3 cups green chile sauce (pages 30–32), or 1 28-ounce can green chile enchilada sauce
1 cup (½ pint) sour cream
4 green onions, chopped
Cilantro sprigs for garnish

1. Heat 2 tablespoons oil in a skillet over medium heat and sauté 1 cup chopped onion until soft and transparent. Remove onions to drain on a paper towel.
2. Heat remaining oil in skillet to medium hot and soft-fry tortillas, one at a time, until limp.
3. Fill each tortilla with ¼ cup cheese, 2 tablespoons onion, and 1 teaspoon chiles. Roll up and place seam side down in a 9 × 13-inch baking dish.
4. Pour sauce over enchiladas.
5. Top with remaining cheese.
6. Bake in a 350°F oven for 10 minutes, or until bubbly.
7. Garnish with sour cream, green onions, and cilantro.

YIELD: *Serves 4 to 6*

VARIATIONS: Add shredded chicken filling (page 16) or pork filling (page 20).

Me gustan estas enchiladas.
I like these enchiladas.

"Enchiladas together with tamales are the traditional foods of the Mexican Indians. The early Spanish colonists of the Pacific coast of America improved these dishes to suit their taste. No boda [wedding] was complete without them. The true enchilada contains no meat and so was used in the meatless menus."
—ANA BEGUÉ DE PACKMAN
Early California Hospitality

Cooking sauces are endlessly adaptable and versatile. Use a thick paste to marinate pork or chicken. Thin it down with broth or water for enchiladas and for moistening fillings. In Santa Fe, almost every tortilla dish is laced with sauce. The only question when eating out is: *Red?* or *green?*

Classic Red Enchiladas

PREPARATION TIME: *30 minutes*
COOKING TIME: *10 minutes*
TOTAL TIME: *40 minutes*

2	tablespoons vegetable oil (with an additional 4 tablespoons oil if you choose corn tortillas)
2	medium onions, finely chopped
3	cups red chile sauce (pages 26–29) or canned enchilada sauce
8 to 10	flour or corn tortillas
2¼	cups (9 ounces) shredded Cheddar cheese
1	2¼-ounce can chopped black olives
½	cup sour cream (optional garnish)

1. Heat 2 tablespoons oil in a skillet over medium heat. Sauté onions until soft and transparent, stirring often. Remove onions to drain on a paper towel.
2. Warm red chile sauce and coat bottom of 9 × 13-inch baking dish with 3 tablespoons sauce.
3. For corn tortillas: Heat remaining 4 tablespoons oil in a skillet on medium heat. Soft-fry the tortillas one at a time, turning once. For flour tortillas, omit the soft-fry process.
4. Dip 1 tortilla at a time into the sauce, then place on a large plate.
5. Spoon ¼ cup cheese, 2 tablespoons onion, and 1 tablespoon olives down the center of the tortilla.
6. Roll up from one side, gently placing each enchilada seam side down in the 9 × 13-inch baking dish.
7. Repeat with remaining tortillas, saving ¼ cup cheese for garnish.
8. Pour remaining sauce over enchiladas, making sure edges are covered.
9. Bake at 350°F for 10 minutes, or until cheese melts.

10. Sprinkle ¼ cup grated cheese as garnish on the top during the last few minutes. Do not allow to dry out.
11. Serve garnished with sour cream.

YIELD: *Serves 4 to 6*

VARIATIONS:

Use a combination of Jack and Cheddar cheeses.

Basic meat fillings could be stuffed into these delicate rolls of cheese oozing with red sauce.

See Stacked Red Enchiladas, page 54.

Combine cheese, onion, and olive mixture with 1 pound fried chorizo or a combination of ½ chorizo, ½ ground beef.

Sauté onions in olive oil.

Skip soft-fry step to eliminate fat. You will need extra sauce as the tortillas will absorb more. The flavor will be about the same but the texture will tend to be spongy.

Sour Cream Enchiladas

PREPARATION TIME: *15 minutes*
COOKING TIME: *15 minutes*
TOTAL TIME: *30 minutes*

2½	cups sour cream
1½	cups chopped green onions, including tops
½	teaspoon ground cumin
2½	cups (10 ounces) shredded sharp Cheddar cheese
4	tablespoons vegetable oil
12	corn tortillas
2	cups red chile sauce (pages 26–29), or
	1½ 10-ounce cans enchilada sauce

TOPPING:

½	cup sour cream
½	cup chopped green onions

1. Combine sour cream, green onions, cumin, and 2 cups of the cheese.
2. Heat oil in a skillet over medium-high heat and soft-fry tortillas one at a time, turning once, until limp.
3. Dip each tortilla in red chile sauce.
4. Place about ¼ cup of the sour cream mixture onto each tortilla.
5. Roll up and place seam side down in a 9 × 13-inch baking dish.
6. Repeat until all tortillas and filling are used and pour remaining sauce over enchiladas.
7. Sprinkle remaining cheese evenly over the top.
8. Bake, uncovered, in a 350°F oven for 15 minutes.
9. Serve by topping the dish with the sour cream and green onions.

YIELD: *Serves 4 to 6*

VARIATION: Add any cooked meat filling (pages 16–21).

"El que hambre tiene, en tortillas piensa. When a person is hungry, they only think about tortillas."
—MEXICAN-AMERICAN PROVERB

"In Juchitán, Oaxaca, the tortillas approach ¼-inch thickness and are slapped onto the inside wall of a hot, barrel-shaped, clay oven and baked. There is nothing to compare to their earthy, slightly smoky taste when they're retrieved from the oven; certainly they are the most unusual tortillas I know in Mexico."
—RICK BAYLESS AND DEANN GROEN BAYLESS
Authentic Mexican

"The Spaniards in Mexico, through necessity, acquired a taste for the corn tortilla which took the place of the oven-baked bread of their old home."
—ANA BEGUÉ DE PACKMAN
Early California Hospitality

Shredded Beef Enchiladas

PREPARATION TIME: *25 minutes*
COOKING TIME: *10 minutes*
TOTAL TIME: *35 minutes*

2	tablespoons vegetable oil
1	medium onion, chopped
2	tablespoons flour
1½	cups sour cream
2	7-ounce cans diced green chiles, drained
1	teaspoon ground cumin
2½	cups (10 ounces) shredded Jack cheese
8 to 10	flour tortillas, softened
3	cups shredded beef filling (page 18)

1. Heat oil in a skillet over medium heat and sauté 1 cup chopped onion until transparent.
2. Stir in flour and cook until it becomes a slightly brown paste.
3. Stir in sour cream, chiles, and cumin and heat until just warm.
4. Remove skillet from heat and stir in 2 cups Jack cheese.
5. Spread 3 tablespoons of sour cream mixture down the center of a tortilla. Top mixture with 2 tablespoons shredded beef and roll up.
6. Place seam side down in a 9 × 13-inch baking dish.
7. Repeat with remaining tortillas and filling.
8. Bake, uncovered, at 350°F for 10 minutes, sprinkling remaining ½ cup Jack cheese over tops of tortillas for last 5 minutes.
9. Serve with salsa, extra sour cream, and remaining chopped onions.

YIELD: *Serves 4 to 6*

VARIATION: Leftover roast beef could be substituted for shredded beef.

"For he who was born to make tamales, even corn husks fall from the sky."
—OLD MEXICAN PROVERB
found in *Conversations with Moctezuma* by Dick J. Reavis

Attempting to appease the conquering Spaniards, Otomí villagers made elaborate preparation. "Everything was at hand, everything was arranged for them: the food, the turkeys, etc. They gave the Spaniards great contentment and went among them quite peacefully. They gave them all they asked for: fodder for the deer they rode, that is, the horses; water; degrained corn, ears of corn, raw, cooked, roasted; green corn tortillas and tamales; squashes cut in sections. They kept pressing these upon them, wishing to become their friends."
—FRAY BERNARDINO DE SAHAGÚN
The War of Conquest

Ground Beef Enchiladas

PREPARATION TIME: *15 minutes*
COOKING TIME: *15 minutes*
TOTAL TIME: *30 minutes*

12   corn tortillas

SAUCE:
  2   tablespoons vegetable oil
  ½   medium onion, chopped
  1   garlic clove, minced
  1   15-ounce can tomato sauce
  2   cups water
  2   beef bouillon cubes
  ¼   teaspoon salt
  1   teaspoon chili powder

FILLING & TOPPING:
  1   pound ground beef
  1   medium onion, chopped
  2   teaspoons chili powder
  ½   teaspoon salt
  2   cups (8 ounces) shredded Cheddar cheese

1. Heat oil in a saucepan over medium heat and sauté onion and garlic until transparent.
2. Add remaining sauce ingredients and bring to a boil over medium-high heat. Reduce heat and simmer for 10 minutes.
3. Brown beef in skillet over medium heat and pour off excess fat.
4. Add half the onion, chili powder, and salt to the browned meat and sauté until onions are transparent, about 5 minutes.
5. Soften tortillas by dipping one at a time in hot sauce.
6. Spoon ¼ cup beef mixture and 2 tablespoons cheese onto each tortilla. Roll up and place seam side down in a 9 × 13-inch baking dish.

7. Cover with remaining sauce. Sprinkle with remaining onion and cheese.
8. Bake, uncovered, at 350°F for 15 minutes, or until cheese melts.

VARIATIONS: Add any of the following or substitute them for the beef: 1 12-ounce can corn with peppers, drained; 1 16-ounce can kidney beans, drained; 1 2¼-ounce can chopped or sliced ripe olives. Substitute ground beef filling (page 21).

YIELD: *Serves 4 to 6*

"The staple food in all of Mexico is the tortilla, a flat cake of fried grain, but in Mexico south of the 22nd parallel the tortilla is made of corn. In the north, it's made of wheat, a plant from across the Atlantic, unknown in Mexico before the Spaniards came. . . . The flour tortilla is a symbol of the north's distinctiveness: flour ties the region to the essentially European culture of the United States as much as its tortilla form ties it to the Mesoamerican culture of Mexico."
—DICK J. REAVIS
Conversations with Moctezuma

Creamy Green Chile and Chicken Enchiladas

PREPARATION TIME: *30 minutes*
COOKING TIME: *30 minutes*
TOTAL TIME: *1 hour*

1	8-ounce package cream cheese, at room temperature
1	cup heavy cream
2½ to 3	cups cooked and shredded chicken, or shredded chicken filling (page 16)
1	cup chopped green onions
2	cups (8 ounces) shredded Jack cheese
3½	cups green chile sauce (pages 30–32), or 1 28-ounce can green chile enchilada sauce
1	can cream of chicken soup, undiluted
12	8-inch flour tortillas

1. Beat cream cheese and heavy cream together until smooth.
2. Fold in chicken, onions, and cheese, reserving ¼ cup chopped onions and ½ cup shredded cheese for topping.
3. Warm green chile sauce and soup and coat bottom of a 9 × 13-inch baking dish.
4. Dip each tortilla in sauce, spoon ½ cup filling down center, roll up, and place seam side down in baking dish.
5. Repeat until all filling is used.
6. Pour extra sauce over enchiladas.
7. Top with remaining grated cheese and onion.
8. Bake at 350°F for 30 minutes.

YIELD: *Serves 4 to 6*

VARIATION: Substitute canned chicken for shredded chicken.

NOTE: Recipe can be doubled or frozen.

Swiss Enchiladas

PREPARATION TIME: *20 minutes*
COOKING TIME: *15 minutes*
TOTAL TIME: *35 minutes*

4	tablespoons vegetable oil
1	small onion, minced
1	garlic clove, minced
2	cups cooked and shredded turkey or chicken, or coarsely chopped or shredded chicken filling (page 16)
2	medium tomatoes, seeded and chopped
12	corn tortillas
2	cups (8 ounces) shredded Jack cheese
2	chicken bouillon cubes
1	cup heavy cream
	Salt and pepper to taste

1. Heat 1 tablespoon cooking oil in a skillet and sauté onions and garlic until transparent, about 5 minutes.
2. Stir in meat and tomatoes and simmer an additional 5 minutes, reducing liquid. Add salt and pepper.
3. Heat remaining oil in another skillet over medium-high and soft-fry tortillas one at a time, turning once, until limp.
4. Spoon ¼ cup of the meat mixture down the middle of each tortilla, roll up, and place seam side down in a lightly greased 9 × 13-inch baking dish.
5. Top thoroughly with cheese.
6. Dissolve bouillon cubes in cream in a double boiler or microwave and pour over enchiladas, making sure edges are covered.
7. Bake at 350°F for 15 minutes.

YIELD: *Serves 4 to 6*

"Almuerza mucho, come más, cena poco y viviras. Eat a lot for breakfast, more at lunch, a little at dinner, and you will live."
—MEXICAN-AMERICAN PROVERB

This is a mellow enchilada with Jack cheese, no chiles, and heavy cream in place of sour cream. Surprise! No Swiss cheese. Perhaps this was first created by a homesick Swiss traveler to Mexico craving a mild dish including dairy products similar to those used in his or her native cuisine.

When ordering enchiladas at a Santa Fe restaurant, you will be asked, "rolled or flat?" and "red or green?" or "with or without an egg?"
—A TOURIST'S OBSERVATION

The *chiquihuite* is the traditional, square-shaped tortilla basket made of woven reed grass. It is lined with a cloth, which must completely cover the tortillas to keep them warm and soft. Never, never leave them uncovered when you help yourself to a tortilla at the table!

Crab and Rice Enchiladas

PREPARATION TIME: *40 minutes*
COOKING TIME: *35 minutes*
TOTAL TIME: *1 hour, 10 minutes*

1	cup rice
6	ounces fresh or frozen crabmeat, thawed and diced
¼	cup chopped green onion
2	cups (8 ounces) shredded Jack cheese
2½	cups red chile sauce (pages 26–29), or 2 10-ounce cans enchilada sauce
⅓	cup vegetable oil
16	corn tortillas
1	cup sour cream
	Ripe olives, sliced for garnish

1. Cook rice according to package directions.
2. Stir crabmeat, onions, 1 cup cheese, and 3 tablespoons red chile sauce into cooked rice.
3. Heat oil in a skillet over medium heat, soft-fry tortillas, and drain on paper towels.
4. Spread each tortilla with ½ cup rice mixture and roll up.
5. Arrange seam side down in a 9 × 13-inch baking dish.
6. Pour remaining sauce over enchiladas.
7. Cover with foil and bake at 350°F for 25 minutes.
8. Sprinkle remaining cheese over top of enchiladas and return to oven, uncovered, for 5 minutes, or until cheese has melted.
9. Top with sour cream and olives before serving.

YIELD: *Serves 6 to 8*

NOTE: Do not use imitation crabmeat.

Crockpot Enchiladas

PREPARATION TIME: *10 minutes*
COOKING TIME: *6 to 8 hours*
TOTAL TIME: *6 to 8 hours*

1½ pounds ground beef
1 medium onion, chopped
1 garlic clove, minced
½ teaspoon salt
½ teaspoon pepper
6 corn tortillas
2 cups fresh or frozen corn kernels, or 1 15-ounce can corn
3 cups red chile sauce (pages 26–29), or 1 19-ounce can enchilada sauce
2 cups (8 ounces) shredded Cheddar cheese
1 2¼-ounce can sliced ripe olives, drained
1 cup sour cream or guacamole (page 39)

1. Brown ground beef and drain.
2. Add onion and garlic and cook over medium heat until tender and transparent.
3. Add salt and pepper.
4. Place 2 tortillas in bottom of a 3 to 4-quart Crockpot.
5. Place a third of the following in layers over the tortillas: meat, corn, sauce, cheese, and olives.
6. Repeat tortillas and other layers two times.
7. Cover and cook on low 6 to 8 hours.
8. Serve with sour cream or guacamole.

YIELD: *Serves 6 to 8*

VARIATIONS:
Oven method: Cook, covered, in a 375°F oven for 30 minutes.
Substitute kidney beans for corn.

Montezuma was referred to as the Great Montezuma by the enslaved Indians who served him lavishly. One description recorded by Díaz of the way he was treated: "Four very beautiful cleanly women brought water for his hands in a sort of deep basin . . . and they held others like plates below to catch the water, and they brought him towels. And two other women brought him tortilla bread, and as soon as he began to eat they placed before him a sort of wooden screen painted over with gold, so that no one should watch him eating."
—BERNAL DÍAZ DEL CASTILLO
The Discovery and Conquest of Mexico, 1517–1521

"Each meal should be a sacramental feast . . . for all we eat doth come of sacrifice."
—JOHN OXENHAM
The Fiery Cross

Garlic, which originated in the Mediterranean long before the birth of Christ and was brought to the New World by Europeans, is now deeply integral to Mexican cooking."
—PATRICIA QUINTANA WITH CAROL HARALSON
Mexico's Feasts of Life

Stacked Red Enchiladas

PREPARATION TIME: *10 minutes*
COOKING TIME: *10 minutes*
TOTAL TIME: *20 minutes*

18   corn or blue-corn tortillas
     Vegetable oil
2½   cups red chile sauce (pages 26–29), or 2 10-ounce cans
     enchilada sauce
 2   small onions, chopped
 3   cups (12 ounces) shredded Cheddar cheese

OPTIONAL CONDIMENTS:
     Sour cream
     Chopped onions
     Chopped or sliced ripe olives
     Green onions
     Salsa
     Shredded lettuce
     Chopped tomato
     Fried eggs

1. Soft-fry the tortillas in vegetable oil.
2. Heat red chile sauce and dip the tortillas, one at a time.
3. Place a sauced tortilla on each of 6 ovenproof plates or a
   baking sheet, preparing to make 6 stacks.
4. Sprinkle 1 tablespoon each onions, cheese, and red chile
   sauce on each tortilla.
5. Repeat the process twice, forming 6 stacks of 3 tortillas
   each.
6. Pour remaining sauce over the stacks and top with
   cheese.
7. Bake at 350°F for 10 minutes, or until cheese melts.
   Serve with condiments.

YIELD: *Serves 6*

"We, although there are many of us, are one single body, for we all share in one loaf."
—I CORINTHIANS
   10:16–17
   Holy Bible

Stacked enchiladas are at home in Santa Fe, their city of origin. They look like a short stack of pancakes, with sauce and filling sandwiched between the tortilla layers. To experience a truly authentic New Mexican taste treat, use blue-corn tortillas and top each stack with a fried egg, sunny-side up!

"Using blue-corn tortillas is the touch that makes an *enchilada* New Mexican, though you will neither gain nor lose in flavor by choosing these . . . I do not recommend it to beginners . . . the commercial blue-corn tortillas, which are tougher than home made ones, already have a perilous tendency to fall apart as they are being dipped."
—HUNTLEY DENT
   The Feast of Santa Fe

VARIATIONS:

Add ground beef: Sauté 1 pound ground beef with the onion and season with ½ teaspoon garlic powder and 1 tablespoon chili powder.

Add shredded chicken filling (page 16).

Add green chiles or sliced ripe olives to layers.

Substitute green sauce (pages 30–32) for red.

Make several tall stacks and cut into wedges to serve. Increase baking time to 15 to 20 minutes.

Chicken Flautas

PREPARATION TIME: *5 minutes*
COOKING TIME: *5 minutes*
TOTAL TIME: *10 minutes*

1½ cups shredded chicken filling (page 16)
  1 cup purchased or homemade salsa picante (page 33)
  8 9-inch flour tortillas, softened
    Vegetable oil
  1 cup guacamole (page 39)

1. Warm chicken filling with ¼ cup salsa in a saucepan or skillet.
2. Spoon 2 to 3 tablespoons filling down center of each tortilla, roll up tightly in a flute shape, and secure with a toothpick.
3. Pour ½ inch oil into a large skillet over medium-high heat.
4. Fry each flauta, turning once, until golden brown and crisp.
5. Drain on paper towels and remove toothpicks.
6. Serve with remaining salsa and guacamole.

YIELD: *Serves 4 to 6*

VARIATION: To make giant flautas, overlap 2 tortillas by 4 inches, spoon filling down center of each pair, roll up, and fry.

Quick Turkey Roll-Ups

PREPARATION TIME: *10 minutes*
COOKING TIME: *10 minutes*
TOTAL TIME: *20 minutes*

1   pound ground raw turkey
¼   cup chopped onion
¼   cup chopped green pepper
1   15-ounce can Mexican-style corn, drained
½   cup prepared taco sauce or salsa picante (page 33)
8   9-inch flour tortillas, softened
½   cup (2 ounces) shredded Cheddar cheese
1   2¼-ounce can sliced ripe olives

1. Crumble turkey into a skillet and cook over medium heat until no longer pink.
2. Add onion and pepper to skillet and cook over medium heat until tender, 5 minutes.
3. Add corn, ½ cup taco sauce, half the olives, and heat.
4. Place ¼ cup filling down center of each tortilla, roll up, and place seam side down in a 9 × 13-inch baking dish.
5. Repeat with remaining tortillas and filling.
6. Pour remaining taco sauce over roll-ups and sprinkle with cheese and olives.
7. Bake at 350°F for 10 minutes, or until cheese melts.

YIELD: *Serves 4 to 6*

VARIATIONS: Substitute corn tortillas for flour; frozen corn, cooked and drained, for canned corn; lean ground beef for turkey.

"If you eat with your eyes as well as your mouth . . . [reading this recipe] will have you salivating."
—*The Oregonian Foodday* August 11, 1992

"On her stone *metate*, Zochee constantly ground corn soaked in lime water to make a dough which she patted into tortillas or rolled around meat and seafood to make a *tamal* or *charupa*."
—from a sixteenth-century story reported by George C. Booth in *The Food & Drink of Mexico*

"The diet of the north is more than a question of taste and convenience. It's a question of culture, class, and caste. The elaboration of corn is the basis of dozens of local cuisines. Mexico has evolved 124 different ways of preparing corn on the cob, 166 types of tortilla, 86 kinds of tamale, more than 100 puddings, pastries, and candies of corn, and 17 different corn-based drinks."
—DICK J. REAVIS *Conversations with Moctezuma*

These goodies wrapped up in a tortilla provide a yummy lunch or snack to be tucked away in a backpack or brown bag. Fillings are as endless as what you find in your refrigerator, or nearest deli or supermarket.

Long ago, when it came time for a picnic dinner, the necessities of laughter, singing, shade trees, a creek, and tasty food were no different than today, with this distinction: "Spanish Californians stand beside a shallow pit filled with rosy embers and hold down sizzling meat-laced skewers. Indios and Indias shake out and lay a cloth upon which to spread the feast. No plates; a large tortilla wrapped around a broiled morsel, another tortilla holding a ladle of frijoles, and a dipperful of piquant sarsa is still a king's feast."
—ANA BEGUÉ DE PACKMAN
Early California Hospitality

Picnic Roll-Ups

(OR, AS APPETIZERS, PARTY PINWHEELS)

PREPARATION TIME: *10 minutes*
COOKING TIME: *0 minutes*
TOTAL TIME: *2 hours to all day*

    One recipe of the filling of your choice: ham, turkey, beef, or vegetarian
6 9-inch flour tortillas (or substitute whole wheat, especially for vegetarian filling)
½ head romaine lettuce, very finely slivered
½ pound thinly sliced ham, turkey, or beef, depending on which filling you choose

HAM FILLING:
8 ounces whipped cream cheese
½ teaspoon Dijon mustard
¾ cup (3 ounces) shredded Swiss cheese
¼ cup finely diced pickles (your choice of dill or sweet)
½ cup finely diced water chestnuts

TURKEY FILLING:
8 ounces whipped cream cheese
1 celery stalk, finely minced
½ cup cranberry sauce
½ cup finely chopped walnuts

BEEF FILLING:
8 ounces whipped cream cheese
½ teaspoon Dijon mustard
    Liquid pepper sauce, to taste
    Freshly ground pepper, to taste
3 green onions, minced
2 tablespoons canned diced green chiles
6 stuffed green olives, minced, or 6 ripe olives, minced
¼ cup finely chopped red onion (optional)

VEGETARIAN FILLING:

- 8 ounces whipped cream cheese
- 1 cup crushed pineapple, thoroughly drained
- 1 cup shredded carrots
- 1 cup raisins
- ½ cup finely chopped walnuts
- ½ cup sunflower seeds

1. Blend together all filling ingredients in a large bowl.
2. Spread 3 tablespoons filling mixture within ½ inch of edges of each tortilla.
3. Spread and press 4 tablespoons lettuce into filling mixture.
4. Cover lettuce with one layer of ham, turkey, or beef (use only lettuce for vegetarian).
5. Roll up each tortilla tightly and wrap tightly in plastic wrap.
6. Chill for 2 hours, all day, or overnight.
7. Serve roll-ups as is or trim each end and cut into 1-inch slices. Serve on a plate of finely slivered lettuce.

YIELD: *6 roll-ups or 30 appetizers*

Ham and Turkey Crepes

PREPARATION TIME: *10 minutes*
COOKING TIME: *15 minutes*
TOTAL TIME: *25 minutes*

4	cups coarsely ground cooked turkey
2	cups coarsely ground cooked ham
2	cups sour cream
1¼	cups red chile sauce (pages 26–29), or 1 10-ounce can enchilada sauce
1	teaspoon ground cumin
1½	cups (6 ounces) shredded sharp Cheddar cheese
1½	cups chopped green onions, including tops
12	9-inch flour tortillas, softened
1	cup salsa picante (page 33), or 8 ounces canned

GARNISH:

1	cup salsa picante (page 33), or 8 ounces canned
½	cup chopped green onions
½	cup shredded sharp Cheddar cheese
½	cup sour cream

1. Combine the turkey, ham, sour cream, chile sauce, cumin, cheese, and green onions.
2. Place ½ cup of the combined mixture in a soft flour tortilla. Roll up and place seam side down in a greased 9 × 13-inch baking dish.
3. Repeat until all tortillas and remaining mixture are used. Pour salsa over crepes.
4. Bake, covered, at 350°F for 15 minutes.
5. Serve with extra salsa, onions, sour cream, and cheese.

YIELD: *Serves 4 to 6*

Ham Roll-Ups

PREPARATION TIME: *15 minutes*
COOKING TIME: *45 minutes*
TOTAL TIME: *1 hour*

¼   pound butter (1 stick)
½   cup flour
1   quart milk
3   cups (12 ounces) shredded Cheddar cheese
1   teaspoon prepared mustard
½   teaspoon salt
¼   teaspoon pepper
12   thin slices of ham
1   pound Jack cheese, cut into ½-inch strips
1   7-ounce can green chiles, cut into ¼-inch strips
12   9-inch flour tortillas, softened
¼   teaspoon paprika

1. Melt butter in a saucepan over low heat.
2. Blend in flour and cook over low heat until smooth and bubbly.
3. Remove saucepan from heat and stir in milk.
4. Return to heat and bring to a boil, stirring constantly.
5. Boil 1 minute.
6. Stir in Cheddar cheese, mustard, salt, and pepper until smooth. Remove from heat.
7. Place 1 piece of ham, Jack cheese, and chile strips in center of each tortilla and roll up.
8. Place seam side down in a greased 9 × 13-inch baking dish.
9. Cover with sauce, sprinkle with paprika, and bake at 350°F for 45 minutes.

YIELD: *Serves 6*

"My mother and other ladies were eager to see that all of the guests were served, and there was always a special plate for a special friend."
—EDNA LEWIS
The Taste of Country Cooking

In Spain, the word *tortilla* is the diminutive of *torta*, the word for cake, and refers to a cold omelet.

"The one thing modernization can't promise though, is the same thick tenderness of tortillas patted by well-practiced hands. It has been done the same way for centuries: She pinches off a nut of fresh, soft *masa* and begins to clap it from one damp hand to the other, those fingers held stiff, with the slightest cup and spring to the palm. Clap and turn, clap and turn, until the malleable *masa* has been coaxed to a thin, even, saucer size."
—RICK BAYLESS AND DEANN GROEN BAYLESS
Authentic Mexican

Donkey Tails

PREPARATION TIME: *10 minutes*
COOKING TIME: *20 minutes*
TOTAL TIME: *30 minutes*

⅔   cup prepared mustard
⅓   cup salsa picante (page 33) or purchased taco sauce
8   hot dogs
8   slices American cheese, each cut into 4 strips
8   9-inch flour tortillas
    Oil for deep-frying

1. Combine mustard and salsa.
2. Cut deep slits in each hot dog; stuff each with 4 strips of cheese.
3. Wrap each hot dog in a tortilla and secure ends with toothpicks.
4. Heat oil in a deep-fat fryer to 375°F and fry wrapped hot dogs, a few at a time. Cook for 2 to 3 minutes, or until tortillas are puffed and golden.
5. Drain well on paper towels.
6. Serve immediately with sauce.

YIELD: *Serves 4 to 6*

VARIATION: After frying, cut up and spear pieces with toothpicks. They make great appetizers.

Taquitos

PREPARATION TIME: *10 minutes*
COOKING TIME: *5 minutes*
TOTAL TIME: *15 minutes*

1½ cups shredded beef filling (page 18)
12 corn tortillas, softened
Vegetable oil
2 cups guacamole (page 39)

1. Place 2 tablespoons filling along one side of each tortilla.
2. Roll up tightly and secure seam with toothpick.
3. Repeat with remaining tortillas and filling.
4. Heat ¼ inch oil in a hot skillet.
5. Place taquitos in oil with toothpick sticking straight up. Fry for a few seconds.
6. Remove toothpick and gently roll over and fry for a few seconds more.
7. Drain on paper towels and serve with guacamole.

YIELD: *Serves 6 to 8 as snack or appetizer*

VARIATIONS:
Use a deep-fat fryer for cooking.
Optional garnishes: Sour cream, salsa, shredded lettuce.
Other fillings: Chicken, turkey, ham, luncheon meat, pork, cheese.

NOTE: Taquitos can be made ahead or frozen and reheated in a 350°F oven until heated through, taking 10 to 20 minutes.

When you are thrilled about a dish, say *"Es muy rico!"*

Taquitos are little tacos. They are rolled tightly, fried quickly, and presented with guacamole as a popular appetizer or snack.

"By some sort of unknown trial and error method, the Mayas, Aztecs, and North American Indians determined that boiling corn in a solution of water and ashes from the fire improved it as a source of vitamins. Of course, they had never heard of vitamins or pellagra, but their cooking method removed the hull more easily, making the corn more digestible. The corn also reacted chemically with the lime in the ashes to make amino acids more readily available to the body, and the lime also released chemically bound niacin, which the body could now utilize."
—DAVE DEWITT AND
  NANCY GERLACH
  Just North of the Border

Chicken Picadillo

PREPARATION TIME: *20 minutes*
COOKING TIME: *10 minutes*
TOTAL TIME: *30 minutes*

1	16-ounce can stewed tomatoes, with liquid
1½	cups salsa picante (page 33), or 12 ounces canned
3	cups shredded chicken filling (about 2 whole breasts) (page 16)
1	red bell pepper, chopped
½	cup raisins
¼	cup slivered almonds, toasted and coarsely chopped
¼	teaspoon ground cinnamon
¼	teaspoon ground cloves
1	teaspoon vinegar
1	garlic clove, minced
8	9-inch flour tortillas, softened
1½	cups (6 ounces) shredded Jack cheese

OPTIONAL GARNISHES:
Sliced ripe olives
Sour cream
Chopped tomatoes
Shredded lettuce

1. Break up tomatoes and combine in a skillet with ¾ cup salsa, the chicken, red bell pepper, raisins, almonds, cinnamon, cloves, vinegar, and garlic.
2. Bring to a boil over medium-high heat, reduce heat, and simmer, uncovered, for 10 minutes, or until liquid is absorbed.
3. Grease a 9 × 13-inch baking dish.
4. Spoon ⅓ cup chicken mixture down the center of a tortilla.
5. Roll up and place seam side down in prepared baking dish.
6. Repeat with remaining tortillas and filling.
7. Spoon remaining ¾ cup salsa picante over tortillas.

8. Cover with foil and bake at 350°F for 8 minutes.
9. Remove foil, sprinkle with cheese, and bake, uncovered, for another 2 minutes.
10. Garnish as desired. Provide additional salsa picante.

YIELD: *Serves 4 to 6*

VARIATIONS:
  Use as filling for burritos or soft tacos.
  Add Mexican or brown rice to the filling.

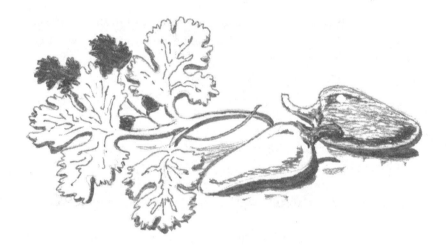

Tortilla Apple Strudel

PREPARATION TIME: *15 minutes*
COOKING TIME: *15 minutes*
TOTAL TIME: *30 minutes*

8	6-inch flour tortillas
2	cups finely chopped apples
¼	cup chopped walnuts
¼	cup raisins (optional)
¼	cup sugar
1	teaspoon ground cinnamon
4	tablespoons butter, melted

1. Crisp 2 tortillas by baking on rack in oven at 450°F for 2 to 3 minutes, or by placing each tortilla between two paper towels and microwaving them on high for 2 minutes.
2. Place crisp tortillas in a double plastic bag and crush with a rolling pin into fine crumbs. Set aside.
3. Mix apples, walnuts, and raisins in a large bowl.
4. Combine sugar and cinnamon in a separate bowl and set aside 2 tablespoons for topping.
5. Combine sugar mixture with apple mixture.
6. Brush tortilla with melted butter and sprinkle with tortilla crumbs.
7. Spread with ¼ cup apple mixture and roll up.
8. Brush outside with butter and place seam side down on baking sheet.
9. Repeat with remaining tortillas and filling.
10. Sprinkle tops with reserved sugar mixture.
11. Bake at 350°F for 15 minutes, or until crisp and slightly brown.

YIELD: *Serves 6*

NOTE: Can be frozen.

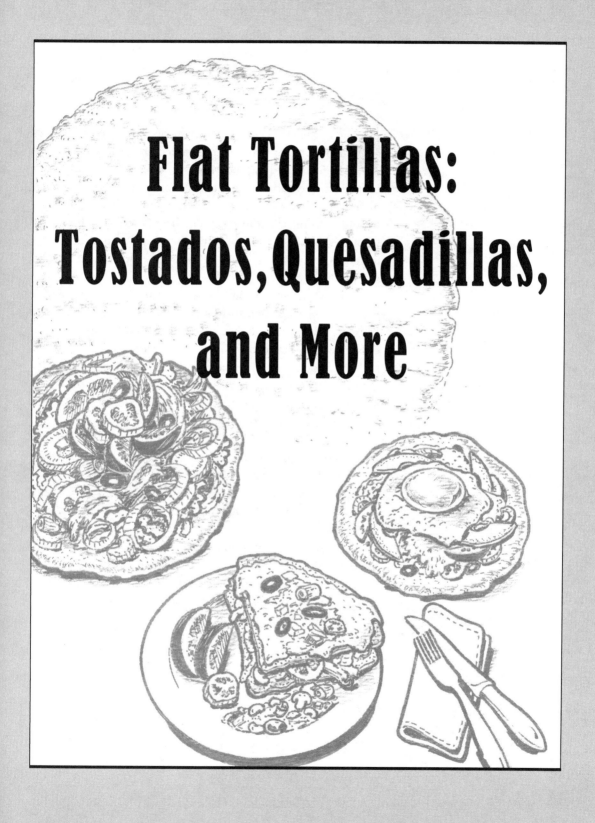

Flat Tortillas:
Tostados, Quesadillas, and More

One of the simplest snacks or meals in Mexico is the tostada—or *chalupa*, as it is called in parts of northern Mexico and along the Mexico/U.S.A. border. In its most basic form a tostada is a whole corn tortilla that is first toasted or fried until crisp around the edges, then piled high with a variety of things including meat, beans, lettuce, cheese, or whatever calls out from the refrigerator. It is a quick and easy, delicious, nutritious, and fun-to-eat, open-face tortilla sandwich.

The word *quesadilla* comes from a combination of the Spanish word, *queso*, which means cheese, and the ending of the word *tortilla*. It is just that simple. Quesadillas are versatile enough to be made open-faced and served as a snack, or stuffed, folded, and drenched in sauce for a full meal. They are the equivalent of our American grilled cheese or the Spanish empanadas. In Mexico, they are often made of raw tortilla dough and fried in lard.

We hope that the recipes in this chapter will inspire you to look at the simple flat tortilla in new, creative ways. Surprise your family some weekend with a brunch of Huevos Rancheros, or a new way to do a salad, either Cobb or Topopo. If pizzas are a family favorite, work up a new twist and substitute a tortilla for the typical bread crust and try out the Presto Pesto Pizza or the Layered Mexican Pizza. If you are looking for something you can do ahead and forget about until dinner time, soak up your tortillas in a Crockpot and try out Crocked Tortillas with Chicken and Beans. Who says there isn't anything new under the sun when you have a flat tortilla ready to go!

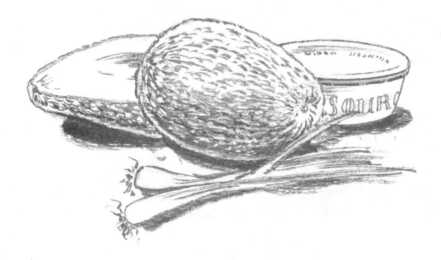

How to Eat a Tostada: The tostada provides an edible plate and is finger food at its best and messiest. Pick the whole thing up like a slice of pizza, but you'll probably need both hands. You may end up with sour cream on your nose, beans on your face, and sauce oozing down your fingers, but you'll have a sensuously good time.

Tostada

PREPARATION TIME: *10 minutes*
COOKING TIME: *0 minutes*
TOTAL TIME: *10 minutes*

6 corn tortillas, fried crisp around the edges and golden brown but not hard toward the center (page 10)
2 cups heated refried beans (page 22), or 1 16-ounce can refried beans
½ cup (2 ounces) shredded Cheddar or Jack cheese
2 cups shredded lettuce
1 medium tomato, chopped

OPTIONAL GARNISHES AND CONDIMENTS:
  Radish slices
  Chopped green onion
  Ripe olive slices
  Whole pickled jalapeño peppers
  Salsa or taco sauce
  Sour cream
  Guacamole or avocado slices

1. Spread each tortilla with an equal amount of beans.
2. Add a layer of cheese, lettuce, and tomato to each tortilla.
3. Offer garnishes at the table or have each diner build his own version from the tortilla up.

YIELD: *Serves 4 to 6*

NOTE: Use stale or dry tortillas for making tostadas as they will not absorb as much oil as a fresh tortilla. Fry them *just right*. If fried too crisp, they will break at first bite, leaving a messy handful.

VARIATIONS:
  Add cooked chicken, turkey, pork, beef, chorizo, ground beef, or cubed potatoes on top of the beans and cheese.

Substitute flour tortilla for corn tortilla, fried into the shape of a cup as for Cobb Salad (page 80).

Add 1 can chile con carne with beans to ground beef filling (page 21) as substitute for refried beans.

Substitute black beans for refried beans and top with tomatillo salsa (page 37) and goat cheese.

Make your own mini tortillas or shape store-bought tortillas with a cookie cutter for mini tostada appetizers.

Stacked ground beef tostada: Layer beans and ground beef on tortilla, top with another tortilla, repeat bean and meat layer, and top with cheese, lettuce, and tomato.

Veggie Tostada: Spread guacamole (page 39) on each tortilla, top with a salad of lettuce, tomato, green onion, cucumbers, radishes, mushrooms, sprouts, etc., tossed with a vinaigrette dressing and sprinkled with mozzarella and Parmesan cheese.

Crab Tostada: Layer crabmeat on top of lettuce layer, garnish with avocado slices, and serve with bottled or homemade green taco sauce or tomatillo salsa (pages 38 and 37).

Stuffed quesadillas look like turnovers. All have cheese in common, are crisp on the outside and warm on the inside. These moon-shaped pockets can be stuffed with the best your refrigerator and imagination allow.

"In Central Mexico the simplest [quesadillas] are filled with some of the braided Oaxaca cheese, a few fresh leaves of [epazote] and strips of peeled *chile poblano* . . . the most highly esteemed [fillings] of all are those of sautéed squash blossoms (*flor de calabaza*) or the ambrosial fungus that grows on the corn (*huitlacoche*)."
—DIANA KENNEDY
The Tortilla Book

Ms. Kennedy also reports that the farther south one goes, the more complicated quesadillas become. One time, a maid of hers made them with cooked potato peelings and a few epazote leaves. "They were delicious."

Quesadilla

PREPARATION TIME: *2 minutes*
COOKING TIME: *8 minutes*
TOTAL TIME: *10 minutes*

1   9-inch flour tortilla
¼   cup (1 ounce) shredded Cheddar cheese

1. Sprinkle tortilla evenly with cheese.
2. Place on an ungreased baking sheet.
3. Bake in 350°F oven until cheese is melted and edges are crisp and brown, about 8 minutes.
4. Cut tortilla into 6 wedges.

YIELD: *Serves 1 as a snack or 6 as appetizers*

VARIATIONS:
Microwave: Place tortilla on a folded paper towel on a microwave-safe plate and cook on high for 1 to 2 minutes, or until cheese melts.
Skillet or griddle: Place tortilla in an ungreased skillet or on griddle and cook on medium-high heat for about 5 minutes, until cheese melts and tortilla is crisp.
Additional ingredients: other cheeses; chopped green onion; taco sauce; chopped tomato; chopped or sliced ripe olives; sliced mushrooms; pinto, black, or refried beans; chopped green chiles, fresh or canned; cooked chorizo; ground beef, chicken, or ham.
Garnishes: sour cream; chopped cilantro; avocado slices; alfalfa sprouts.
Layered: Place another flour tortilla on top of cheese. Turn over to crisp both sides if using skillet method.
Four-cheese-herb: Spread semisoft herb cheese over tortilla, top with thin tomato slices, sprinkle with Parmesan, Swiss, and mozzarella cheese, and microwave on high until melted.
Onion-Brie: Combine Brie with sautéed onions and chopped cilantro, papaya, or mango. Spread on flour tortilla and microwave on high until melted.

Crab-olive: Combine 2 tablespoons crabmeat, 1 tablespoon mayonnaise or salad dressing, 2 drops of hot pepper sauce, 2 tablespoons shredded Jack cheese, 1 tablespoon sliced ripe olives. Spread onto flour tortilla and bake in 350°F oven until melted, about 8 minutes, or microwave on high until melted.

"All common servants in Mexico, and all common people, eat with their fingers! Those who are rather particular, roll up two tortillas, and use them as a knife and fork, which, I can assure you from experience, is a great deal better than nothing, when you have learnt how to use them."
—FRANCES CALDERÓN DE LA BARCA
Life in Mexico, 1838

This south-of-the-border version of a toasted cheese sandwich is quick to make for a satisfying snack, appetizer, lunch, or accompaniment for soup or salad. What could be simpler than a tasty flour tortilla base covered with your favorite cheese melted to perfection. Prepared in the microwave, it is a snack even the youngest chef in your house can make on his own.

Stuffed Quesadilla

PREPARATION TIME: *10 minutes*
COOKING TIME: *15 to 20 minutes*
TOTAL TIME: *25 to 30 minutes*

1   cup (4 ounces) shredded Cheddar cheese
1   cup (4 ounces) shredded Jack cheese
    Butter or margarine
4   9-inch flour tortillas
1   7-ounce can diced green chile peppers, drained
1   medium onion, chopped
2   medium tomatoes, chopped
½   cup salsa picante (page 33) or purchased salsa

1. Mix Cheddar and Jack cheese.
2. Butter one side of a tortilla lightly and place in a large skillet over medium-high heat.
3. Place ½ cup cheese mixture on tortilla.
4. Add 1 to 2 tablespoons chiles, ¼ cup onion, ¼ cup tomato, and 1 to 2 tablespoons salsa.
5. Fry tortilla until slightly crisp on bottom and cheese is melted, then fold.
6. Keep warm in oven set at 200°F.
7. Repeat with remaining tortillas.
8. Serve with extra salsa.

YIELD: *Serves 4*

VARIATIONS:

Oven method: Place tortillas on a baking sheet in a 400°F oven and follow same procedure. Fold before serving.

Additional ingredients: Check your refrigerator for any of a number of leftovers waiting to be included in a quesadilla—vegetables, meats, seafood, chiles, beans of any kind, or even papaya.

Substitute: Whole wheat tortillas for flour.

Microwave directions: High for 2 to 3 minutes, or until the cheese melts. Fold before serving.

Turkey-Stuffed Quesadilla

PREPARATION TIME: *10 minutes*
COOKING TIME: *5 minutes*
TOTAL TIME: *15 minutes*

6   9-inch flour or whole wheat tortillas
2   cups refried beans (page 22), or 1 16-ounce can refried
    beans
1   4-ounce can diced green chiles, drained
1   cup (4 ounces) shredded Jack cheese
1   medium tomato, finely diced
½   teaspoon ground cumin
1   cup finely diced cooked turkey, or 6 thinly sliced pieces
    Butter or margarine

1. Spread each tortilla with 3 tablespoons beans.
2. Sprinkle over half of each tortilla: 1 teaspoon chiles, 2 tablespoons cheese, 1 tablespoon chopped tomato, dash of cumin, 2 tablespoons diced turkey or 1 thin slice.
3. Fold each tortilla, brush both sides lightly with butter, and place on a baking sheet.
4. Broil until lightly browned and crisp, about 2 minutes; turn and brown other side.

YIELD: *Serves 4 to 6*

"When people come together who have not previously met, they are a bit reserved; but when food is introduced there is an immediate change in the atmosphere. The power of the festive table brings a feeling of gentleness and warmth."
—ALAN HOOKER
Vegetarian Gourmet Cookery

"Near Cuernavaca, the cooks fry *quesadillas* filled with shredded chicken, minced pork or beef *picadillo*, and black corn mushrooms (*huitlacoche*), as well as the deliciously pungent brains with *epazote*, and . . . mushrooms with green chile. . . . In Toluca, large *quesadillas* show up with a filling of squash blossoms . . . and on the coasts, crab, shrimp and poached fish find their way into turnovers."
—RICK BAYLESS AND DEANN GROEN BAYLESS
Authentic Mexican

Crunchy Cheese Quesadilla

PREPARATION TIME: *10 minutes*
COOKING TIME: *5 minutes*
TOTAL TIME: *15 minutes*

½ small green pepper, finely chopped
½ small onion, finely chopped
½ medium tomato, finely chopped
1 celery stalk, finely choppped
1 cup (4 ounces) shredded Cheddar cheese
½ teaspoon chili powder
6 corn tortillas

1. Combine vegetables, cheese, and chili powder.
2. Mound equal amount of mixture on each tortilla.
3. Place on a baking sheet and broil until cheese melts.

YIELD: *Serves 4*

VARIATIONS:
  Microwave on high for 2 minutes.
  Substitute flour or whole wheat tortillas for corn tortillas.

"Hospitality consists in a little fire, a little food, and an immense quiet."
—RALPH WALDO EMERSON
Journal, 1856

"In many parts of Mexico [quesadillas] are just filled with strips of Chihuahua cheese, which melts and 'strings' nicely—a Mexican requirement."
—DIANA KENNEDY
The Tortilla Book

Finding herself without food or bed for the night, Frances Calderón de la Barca, in *Life in Mexico, 1938*, describes how two women, "pitying our hungry condition, came to offer their services; one asked me if I should like 'to eat a *burro* in the mean time?' A burro being an *ass*, I was rather startled at the proposition, and assured her that I should infinitely prefer waiting a little longer before resorting to so desperate a measure. 'Some people call them *pecadoras*' (female sinners!) said her sister. Upon this the gentleman came to our assistance, and burros or pecadoras were ordered forthwith. They proved to be hot tortillas, with cheese in them, and we found them particularly good."

Cheese Crisp

PREPARATION TIME: *10 minutes*
COOKING TIME: *15 minutes*
TOTAL TIME: *25 minutes*

Vegetable oil
2   12- or 15-inch flour tortillas
1   cup (4 ounces) shredded Cheddar cheese
1   cup (4 ounces) shredded Jack cheese
¼   cup grated Parmesan cheese
½   cup salsa fresca (page 34)

1. Heat oil in a large skillet or wok to ¼-inch depth on medium-high heat.
2. Fry one tortilla at a time by coating with oil and pushing against sides of pan to form a rim or cup.
3. Tilt pan to coat tortilla rims with oil and fry until crisp.
4. Drain, cup side down, on paper towel and repeat procedure with second tortilla.
5. Cover loosely and store at room temperature for up to 8 hours.
6. Sprinkle each tortilla with half the cheeses and top with half the salsa.
7. Bake in a 350°F oven until cheese melts (5 to 8 minutes).

YIELD: *Serves 4 to 6 snackers*

VARIATIONS:

Substitute asadero, Mexican-style string cheese, for Jack cheese.

Substitute coarsely crumbled catija, Mexican-style dry white cheese, for Parmesan cheese.

Substitute ¼ pound fried chorizo sausage for Parmesan cheese.

Substitute ⅓ cup sliced ripe olives and ⅓ cup canned diced green chiles for salsa and Parmesan.

"Tell me what you eat and I'll tell you what you are."
—JEAN ANTHELME BRILLAT-SAVARIN
The Physiology of Taste,
1759–1794

This snack is made to share. Each person simply reaches in and breaks off chunks to eat out of hand. For the braver souls, offer a shaker filled with pure ground red chile to add a fiery touch to the already sizzling cheese.

"For as long as Ramón and his generation could remember, mothers had kept the same schedule every day. You could set your watch by it. About eight o'clock every night, after supper was served, they put a pot of corn, lime, and water on the hearth to boil. When they arose at sunrise, they strained the corn and washed it of its lime and skins. Then they gathered at the grinding mill. They were back at home by 6:00 A.M., forming tortillas of *masa,* or meal, with their hands. Nobody in Macuil liked the taste, texture, or color of the machine-made tortillas sold in other, bigger towns."
—DICK J. REAVIS
Conversations with Moctezuma

In Mexico, huevos
rancheros would be
appropriate for
almuerzo, the hearty late
breakfast.

From a story recorded
in *The Food & Drink of
Mexico*, by George C.
Booth: "For a breakfast
beverage, [Zochee]
dropped a ball of the
[corn] dough into hot
sweetened water and
served him *atole*, or
whipped cacao and
vanilla into frothy
chocolate."

Huevos Rancheros

PREPARATION TIME: *10 minutes*
COOKING TIME: *10 minutes*
TOTAL TIME: *20 minutes*

4	tablespoons vegetable oil
1	garlic clove, minced
1	medium onion, chopped
1	16-ounce can tomatoes or stewed tomatoes, drained, or 4 fresh tomatoes
2	fresh jalapeño peppers, chopped, or 1 4½-ounce can green chiles, chopped
	Salt to taste
¼	teaspoon dried oregano
¼	teaspoon ground cumin (optional)
4 to 6	corn tortillas
4 to 6	eggs
¼	cup each shredded Jack and Cheddar cheese, combined

1. Heat 2 tablespoons oil in a large skillet.
2. Add garlic and onion; cook until tender.
3. Add tomatoes, jalapeños, salt, oregano, and cumin.
4. Simmer 10 minutes, breaking up large pieces of tomato.
5. Heat remaining oil in another skillet over medium heat and add tortillas, one at a time. Cook, turning once, just until soft (about 5 seconds each side). Drain on paper towels.
6. Break eggs into a saucer and carefully slip, without breaking the yolks, into simmering sauce.
7. Cover and poach until firm (5 to 7 minutes).
8. Place 1 tortilla on each plate and top with egg and sauce.
9. Sprinkle with cheeses and place under broiler (or in microwave) to melt cheese.

YIELD: *Serves 4 to 6*

VARIATIONS:

Eggs: Fry or scramble and cover with sauce.

Sauces: Prepared salsas (pages 33–37) or 1 cup red chile sauce (pages 26–29) plus 1 8-ounce can tomato sauce

Beans: Use 2 cups refried beans (page 22) or 2 cups canned refried or pinto beans. Serve on side or spread on tortilla before adding egg and sauce.

Garnishes: Use 1 or more of the following—avocado slices or guacamole (page 39), fresh cilantro, radishes, green onion, or sour cream.

Casserole form: See page 121.

> "After an enormous number of bulls had been caught and labelled, we went to breakfast. We found a tent prepared for us, formed of bows of trees intertwined with garlands of white moss . . . and beautifully ornamented with red blossoms and scarlet berries. We sat down upon heaps of white moss, softer than any cushion. The Indians had cooked meat under the stones for us, which I found horrible, smelling and tasting of smoke. But we had also boiled fowls, and quantities of burning chile, hot tortillas . . . quantities of fresh tunas, granaditas, bananas, aguacates, and other fruits. . . ."
> —FRANCES CALDERÓN DE LA BARCA
> *Life in Mexico*, 1838

Cobb Salad

PREPARATION TIME: *45 minutes*
COOKING TIME: *0 minutes*
TOTAL TIME: *45 minutes*

Vegetable oil
6   9-inch flour tortillas, softened (page 6)
½   head iceberg lettuce, finely chopped
½   head leafy greens (curly endive, romaine, etc.), finely chopped
½   bunch watercress (optional), finely chopped
1   tablespoon chopped chives (optional)
2   medium tomatoes, diced
3   cups shredded chicken filling (page 16), or 2 chicken breasts, cooked and diced
6   strips bacon, cooked crisp and crumbled
1   large avocado, peeled and diced
½   cup crumbled blue cheese

DRESSING:
⅓   cup red wine vinegar
½   teaspoon sugar
1   tablespoon lemon juice
½   teaspoon salt
½   teaspoon black pepper
1   teaspoon Worcestershire sauce
½   teaspoon dry mustard
1   garlic clove, minced
½   cup olive oil or vegetable oil

1. Heat enough oil to fill a skillet halfway, choosing a skillet slightly smaller than the tortillas.
2. Place pliable tortilla in the hot oil so the sides curl up around the skillet forming a cup. Fry until crisp.
3. Drain and cool tortilla.
4. Repeat with remaining tortillas.
5. Combine all salad ingredients and toss.

"A sensitive approach to food may extend sensitivity almost without effort on our part into other areas of our lives. The art of getting along amicably with neighbors and friends requires true sensitivity, an awareness of all of man's hungers."
—ALAN HOOKER
Vegetarian Gourmet Cookery

This main-dish salad is named after the late Robert A. Cobb, president of the famous Hollywood Brown Derby restaurant. It consists of a combination of ingredients finely chopped and tossed with a French-style dressing, served in a molded tortilla shell.

"Freshly cooked tortillas eaten at the table are usually torn into triangular strips and used to scoop or push food."
—L. PATRICK COYLE, JR.
The World Encyclopedia of Food

6. Combine all dressing ingredients, mix vigorously, and toss with the salad.
7. Serve salad in individual tortilla shells.

YIELD: *Serves 6*

NOTE: Tortillas may be made ahead and crisped in the oven just before serving.

Topopo Salad

PREPARATION TIME: *45 minutes*
COOKING TIME: *0 minutes*
TOTAL TIME: *45 minutes*

4   corn tortillas, crisp-fried (page 6)
2   cups refried beans (page 22), or 1 16-ounce can refried beans
2   cups fresh or frozen peas, cooked
2   fresh jalapeño peppers, seeded and minced
1   cup chopped green onions
½   head iceberg lettuce, finely shredded
½   cup vegetable oil
4   tablespoons red wine vinegar
½   teaspoon salt
½   teaspoon pepper
2   cups shredded chicken filling (page 16), or 2 cups cooked shredded chicken or turkey
2   avocados, peeled, pitted, and sliced lengthwise
¼   cup diced Cheddar cheese
4   tablespoons canned diced green chiles
½   cup grated Parmesan cheese
4   cherry tomatoes or red cherry peppers

1. Spread each tortilla with an equal amount of beans.
2. Toss peas, jalapeño peppers, and green onion with the lettuce.
3. Add oil, vinegar, salt, and pepper to salad and toss.
4. Mound salad onto each tortilla, creating a mountain shape.
5. Alternate meat and avocado slices vertically around the salad.
6. Sprinkle diced cheese and chiles over the salad.
7. Sprinkle Parmesan cheese on top of salad.
8. Top with cherry tomato or pepper.

YIELD: *4 main-dish salads*

Layered Mexican Pizza

PREPARATION TIME: *10 minutes*
COOKING TIME: *5 minutes*
TOTAL TIME: *15 minutes*

12 9-inch flour tortillas
½ pound ground beef filling (page 21), or browned ground beef
2 cups refried beans (page 22), or 1 16-ounce can refried beans
1 cup salsa picante (page 33), or purchased taco sauce
2 cups (½ pound) shredded Jack or Cheddar cheese, or a combination
2 medium tomatoes, finely diced
¼ cup chopped green onions
6 ripe olives, sliced

1. Crisp tortillas on rack in a 450°F oven.
2. Heat ground beef filling in a skillet over medium-high heat.
3. Spread a thin layer of beans on 6 tortillas.
4. Spread ground beef equally over bean layer.
5. Place another tortilla on top of each pizza.
6. Pour sauce over each tortilla.
7. Sprinkle cheese over each pizza and melt briefly in microwave or under broiler.
8. Sprinkle tomatoes and green onions over each pizza.
9. Slice each pizza into quarters and garnish with an olive slice.

YIELD: *Serves 4 to 6, or more as a snack or appetizer*

Buen provecho means eat hearty.

Today, in the Yucatán and Gulf, *tortillerías* pat their tortilla cakes onto a piece of plastic rather than onto a banana leaf.

"At the hand of Cortés, the Spaniards pressed onward into México. After the people of an area called Tecoac perished, the mighty Tlaxcallans knew they were next.
"At a meeting of the rulers, [they] took counsel, weighed the news among themselves, and discussed what to do.
" 'How shall we act?' some asked. 'The only thing to do,' advised still others, 'is to submit to these men, to befriend them, to reconcile ourselves to them. Otherwise, sad would be the fate of the common folk.'
This argument prevailed. The rulers of Tlaxcalla went to meet the Spaniards with food offerings of turkey, eggs, fine white tortillas—the tortillas of lords."
—FRAY BERNARDINO DE SAHAGÚN
The War of Conquest

Presto Tortilla Pizza

"The soul of *pesto* may be basil, but its heart is garlic."
—*The Garlic Lovers' Cookbook Volume II*
The Gilroy Garlic Festival Association, Inc.

Flour tortillas make a great base for instant pizzas. They make delicious snacks, appetizers, or a light lunch, and can be made in multiples for many hearty appetites. Try the toppings suggested or make up your own combinations.

"The use of olive oil is as necessary to true Early California cooking as the use of pure lard in Mexican cuisine. All the missions, and later, most of the ranchos, pressed their own olive oil."
—JACQUELINE HIGUERA McMAHAN
California Rancho Cooking

PREPARATION TIME: *10 minutes*
COOKING TIME: *5 minutes*
TOTAL TIME: *15 minutes*

FRESH TOMATO-PESTO TOPPING:

- 1 9-inch flour tortilla
- 1 cup firmly packed fresh basil
- ½ cup snipped fresh parsley
- ½ cup grated Parmesan cheese
- ¼ cup pine nuts or walnuts
- 2 garlic cloves, crushed
- ¼ cup olive oil
- 1 medium tomato, thinly sliced
     Salt to taste
- 1 ounce mozzarella cheese, thinly sliced

1. Bake tortilla on rack in a 450°F oven until crisp.
2. Prepare pesto by blending or processing basil, parsley, Parmesan, nuts, garlic, and olive oil at high speed until smooth.
3. Place tortilla on a cookie sheet and spread with 3 table-spoons pesto.
4. Arrange sliced tomatoes over pesto.
5. Salt lightly to taste.
6. Top with sliced mozzarella cheese.
7. Place under broiler until cheese begins to melt.
8. Cut into wedges and serve.

YIELD: *Serves 1, or 2 to 3 as appetizers*

VARIATION: To microwave, place tortilla between two paper towels and microwave on high for 2 minutes, or until crisp. Discard paper towels and place tortilla on microwave-safe plate. Arrange pesto, tomato, and cheese as above. Microwave on high for 1 minute, or until cheese begins to melt.

TIP: Pesto can be refrigerated or frozen until ready to use. It may also be served on pasta or bread.

AVOCADO-DILL TOPPING:

1 9-inch flour tortilla
3 tablespoons pizza, spaghetti, or plain tomato sauce (if using plain tomato sauce, sprinkle with ½ teaspoon oregano or Italian seasonings)
¼ avocado, peeled and thinly sliced
½ cup (2 ounces) shredded mozzarella, Jack, or provolone cheese, or a combination
2 tablespoons chopped pecans
2 teaspoons snipped fresh dill or 1 teaspoon dried dill

Follow preparation method for Fresh Tomato-Pesto Topping.

SAUSAGE TOPPING:

1 9-inch flour tortilla
3 tablespoons pizza, spaghetti, or plain tomato sauce (if using plain tomato sauce, sprinkle with ½ teaspoon oregano or Italian seasonings)
⅓ cup (2 ounces) shredded mozzarella, Jack, or provolone cheese, or a combination
⅓ cup sliced pepperoni or cooked and crumbled Italian sausage or a combination
¼ cup grated Parmesan cheese

Follow preparation method for Fresh Tomato-Pesto Topping.

> "Most of the early Spanish farms in the highlands of New Spain (Mexico) raised wheat; in accordance with the policy of the viceroys. The government had to be constantly vigilant to assure that New Spain would produce sufficient supplies of wheat and other foods to feed itself, for close attention to farming was simply not a Castilian virtue."
> —ALFRED W. CROSBY
> *The Columbian Exchange: Biological and Cultural Consequences of 1492*

Crocked Tortillas with Chicken and Beans

PREPARATION TIME: *10 minutes*
COOKING TIME: *6 to 8 hours in Crockpot*
TOTAL TIME: *8 hours*

1　tablespoon vegetable oil
1　medium onion, diced
2　garlic cloves, minced
3　cups shredded chicken filling (page 16)
1¼　cups red chile sauce (pages 26–29), or 1 10-ounce can enchilada sauce
1　8-ounce can tomato sauce
2　16-ounce cans baked beans, BBQ style baked beans, or pinto beans
2　cups fresh or frozen corn kernels, or 1 16-ounce can, drained
8　corn tortillas
2½　cups (10 ounces) shredded Cheddar cheese
1　6-ounce can sliced black olives, drained

1. Heat oil in a medium skillet and sauté onion and garlic until soft and transparent.
2. Remove skillet from heat, add chicken, and mix.
3. Stir together in a large bowl red chile sauce, tomato sauce, beans, and corn.
4. Spray Crockpot with nonstick spray.
5. Place 2 tortillas in bottom of Crockpot.
6. Layer a third of chicken mixture, a third of bean and corn mixture, and a quarter of cheese on top of tortillas.
7. Continue layering two more times.
8. Top with 2 tortillas, remaining cheese, and olives.
9. Cover and cook on low setting for 6 to 8 hours.

YIELD: *Serves 8*

VARIATION: Layer as above in a deep casserole dish. Cover and bake in a 375°F oven for 1 hour.

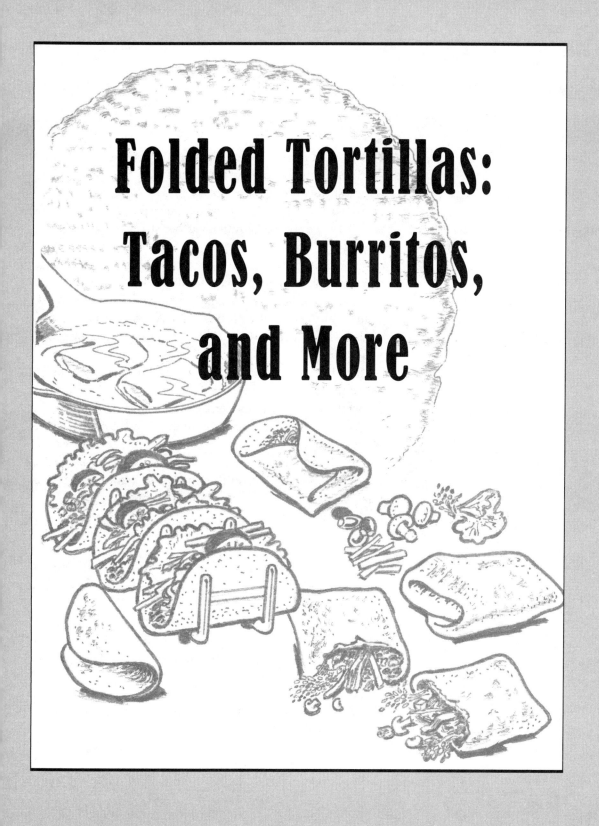

Folded Tortillas:
Tacos, Burritos,
and More

The word *taco*, in Spanish, means snack. In Mexico, millions of fresh tacos are consumed every day. In their simplest form they are hot, soft tortillas rolled around shredded meat or mashed beans and spiced with salsa or sauce. They are readily available from street vendors and are eaten out of the hand.

In the United States, a taco can mean a corn or flour tortilla, rolled or folded, soft or crisp-fried. Typically, however, the American taco is a tortilla that has been crisp-fried into a U shape and then filled with beef, chicken, or beans, and garnished with iceberg lettuce, shredded cheese, diced tomatoes, and salsa.

Much like the American sandwich, the Mexican taco can be as simple or complex as imagination, time, and taste buds allow. It would take a mathematician to come up with all the different kinds of taco variations either south or north of the border—and there are no wrong ways to make one. Tacos can be served for breakfast, lunch, or dinner as well as for snacks, and they can be filled with the simplest of leftover meats and salad ingredients or the most elaborate of fillings for a substantial main dish.

We'll get you started here with a basic ground beef taco, and then move on to tacos with a variety of meat, poultry, fish, and vegetable fillings. Note also that most of the folded tacos in this chapter could also be rolled into a soft taco variation.

The word *burrito*, which means "little donkey" in Spanish, is a flour tortilla that has been warmed and folded into a bundle around a hot filling. When there are no refried beans in the filling, they are referred to as *burros*.

The traditional filling for burritos was just leftover refried beans, and not many of them, giving you the full flour tortilla flavor. Nowadays, the tortillas prosper with half a cup or more of beans, rice, cheese, and meat, too, if that's the gourmet pleasure desired.

Burritos can be eaten from the hand or can become table food requiring a knife and fork if they are smothered with a red or green chile sauce and melted cheese. When burritos are fried crisp, they become chimichangas.

A burrito is different from a soft taco in that it is not simply folded, but folded into a tightly closed bundle, as described below.

HOW TO FOLD A BURRITO:
1. Place filling just below center of tortilla.
2. Fold bottom of tortilla over filling.
3. Fold left and right sides to center.
4. Fold up to form a tightly closed package.

Basic Ground Beef Tacos

¡No hay reglas fijas!
There are no fixed rules!

Mini tacos make
excellent appetizers. For
extra fun, prepare your
own baby-sized 4-inch
tortillas from the raw
dough (pages 8–11) to
make your own mini
Basic Flour or Corn
Tortillas.

"I have seen Mexicans
stuff a taco with rice,
beans, crumbled
chorizo, shredded
chicken or stewed goat.
In Tehuantepec, a
gourmet finds tacos
filled with delicate
iguana meat. Tampico is
noted for armadillo
tacos and the hardy
mountaineers in the
state of Hidalgo use the
maguey worm."
—GEORGE C. BOOTH
*The Food & Drink of
Mexico*

PREPARATION TIME: *15 to 20 minutes*
COOKING TIME: *15 minutes*
TOTAL TIME: *30 to 35 minutes*

	Vegetable oil
12	corn tortillas, softened
2	cups ground beef filling
2	small tomatoes, chopped
2	cups shredded lettuce
1	cup (4 ounces) shredded Cheddar cheese
1	cup salsa or taco sauce (pages 33–38)

1. Heat ¼ inch oil in a large skillet over medium-high heat.
2. Spoon 2 to 3 tablespoons beef filling down center of each tortilla.
3. Place tortilla flat in skillet and heat slightly until it is flexible enough to fold one side over the filling without tearing or cracking. Use tongs or spatula and fork.
4. Gently press folded side down with tongs until tortilla begins to crisp and holds shape on its own.
5. Repeat with 3 or 4 more tortillas, leaving ample cooking space in skillet.
6. Crisp-fry each taco on one side and, using a spatula and fork or tongs, turn over to crisp remaining side.
7. Arrange tomatoes, lettuce, cheese, and salsa in separate bowls for diners to spoon into tacos as desired.

YIELD: *Serves 4 to 6*

VARIATIONS:

Soft tacos: Warm and soften tortillas, spoon filling down center of each tortilla, garnish as above, fold or roll up, and eat. With some fillings, use 2 tortillas together for a sturdier base. These are easier for a large group or buffet as you simply need to replenish the supply of warm tortillas. This is also a safer method when children are involved in the preparation.

Taco shells: In this less traditional method, tortillas are deep-fried and filled later. Heat ¼ cup vegetable oil in a skillet over medium-high heat. Place tortilla in hot oil, turning once, until softened, about 10 seconds. With tongs, fold tortilla in half holding slightly open; continue to fry and turn once until both sides are crisp. Drain on paper towels, keep warm, and repeat for remaining tortillas.

Rolled tacos: See taquitos (page 63).

Fillings: 2 cups shredded beef, pork, or chicken filling (pages 16–20), chorizo, sliced steak, barbecued chicken, eggs, fish, refried beans, pinto beans, diced potatoes, or a combination that appeals.

Purchase a roasted chicken from the supermarket deli, cut up, and place on a platter or cutting board for each person to tear or shred and place in a tortilla.

Additional garnishes and condiments: Sour cream, avocado slices, chopped or sliced ripe olives, selection of shredded cheeses, chopped green or sweet onion, diced green peppers, sliced jalapeños, fresh cilantro sprigs, cucumber chunks, sliced radishes.

Sauces: Check the shelf at your market or deli for unusual sauces, from mild to very spicy and from thin to chunky. Some stores carry fresh as well as jarred or canned sauces.

Substitute flour for corn tortillas and make giant tacos.

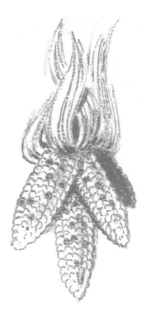

Corn tortillas aren't just for tacos anymore. They are exceptionally low in fat, high in complex carbohydrates, and have no cholesterol. According to the U. S. Department of Agriculture's *Dietary Guidelines for Americans*, we need to "choose a diet low in fat, saturated fat, and cholesterol," and one with "plenty of grain products, using salt and sodium only in moderation." Let's hear it for a corn tortilla!

"From Guadalajara north, tacos are generally folded and fried, frequently with pork inside . . . in Guerrero, there are thin rolled *taquitos* stuffed with ricotta. In Mérida, Yucatán, the cooks fill crisp tortilla tubes (resembling Italian cannoli shells) with ground meat (*codzitos*) and douse them with tomato sauce. Only on the northern border do U-shaped, hamburger-stuffed tacos show up; I think it's clear which way the influence is going."
—RICK BAYLESS AND
 DEANN GROEN
 BAYLESS
 Authentic Mexican

Turkey Tacos

PREPARATION TIME: *5 minutes*
COOKING TIME: *10 minutes*
TOTAL TIME: *15 minutes*

1	tablespoon vegetable oil
½	medium onion, chopped
2	cups cubed cooked turkey
½	cup chopped green onions
1	16-ounce can stewed tomatoes, drained
1	8-ounce can diced green chiles, drained
½	cup chopped walnuts
	Salt to taste
1	cup (4 ounces) shredded medium Cheddar cheese
12	corn tortillas, softened

CONDIMENTS:

Chopped lettuce
Chopped fresh tomatoes
Avocado slices
Sour cream
Guacamole (page 39)

1. **Heat** oil in a skillet over medium-high heat and sauté onion until transparent.
2. Add turkey, green onions, tomatoes, chiles, walnuts, and salt.
3. Bring to a boil, reduce heat, and simmer for about 5 minutes.
4. Place 2 tablespoons meat mixture and 1 tablespoon cheese in each tortilla and fold or crisp-fry as for ground beef taco (page 90).
5. Serve with choice of condiments.

YIELD: *Serves 4 to 6*

Breakfast Tacos

PREPARATION TIME: *2 minutes*
COOKING TIME: *10 minutes*
TOTAL TIME: *12 minutes*

2   tablespoons margarine
1   small onion, chopped
1   garlic clove, chopped
6   eggs, beaten
¼   teaspoon ground cumin
½   cup red chile sauce (pages 26–29) or salsa picante
1   cup (4 ounces) shredded medium Cheddar cheese
6   corn tortillas, softened

1. **Heat** margarine in a skillet over medium heat and sauté onion and garlic until tender.
2. Add eggs, cumin, and ¼ cup salsa.
3. Scramble egg mixture until set.
4. Stir in cheese.
5. Spoon eggs into tortillas, fold, and serve.
6. Pass remaining salsa.

YIELD: *Serves 4*

VARIATION: Add olives, avocados, or green onions, or use tomato sauce as a substitute for the salsa and Jack cheese for the Cheddar.

"You always remember the last taste of anything you eat, and the last bite should leave you with a very happy memory."
—ALAN HOOKER
Vegetarian Gourmet Cookery

"The rancho was self-sufficient by the mid-nineteenth century and, with its *gente de razón* and indios, was reminiscent of feudal times. The rhythm of life was set by the Don, who arose with the lucero, the morning star. After prayer and a cup of hot chocolate, he rode off with his vaqueros to check the cattle. He lived on horseback until he died. The hours of the day were kept by the return of the riders for meals. Around mid-morning, almuerzo would be served—a breakfast of chorizo sausage, fried and accompanied by eggs or mixed with frijoles. There would be refried beans shaped into a thin pancake, a stack of flour tortillas, some red wine, fruit and perhaps coffee made with burnt wheat if coffee beans had not come on the last ship from Mexico."
—JACQUELINE HIGUERA McMAHAN
California Rancho Cooking

Barbecued Chicken Tacos

PREPARATION TIME: *10 minutes*
COOKING TIME: *25 minutes*
TOTAL TIME: *2 hours, 35 minutes*

¼   cup vegetable oil
4   tablespoons (½ stick) butter, melted
1   garlic clove, minced
1   teaspoon onion powder
½   teaspoon ground cumin
1   teaspoon paprika
2   teaspoons lemon juice
1   (2 to 3 pound) chicken, cut into your favorite pieces
12   corn tortillas
1   16-ounce can pinto beans or pintos with chiles
3   cups cabbage salad or coleslaw with oil and vinegar dressing
1   cup salsa fresca (page 34) or purchased salsa

1. Combine oil, butter, garlic, onion powder, cumin, paprika, and lemon juice in a shallow pan or plastic bag.
2. Add chicken to marinade, cover, and marinate several hours or overnight, turning occasionally.
3. Remove chicken from marinade and place on barbecue grill over medium-hot coals.
4. Cook, basting frequently and turning, for about 25 minutes.
5. Warm tortillas by placing on grill and turning once.
6. Shred chicken, or serve pieces for each diner to shred.
7. Place tortillas in palm of hand, fill with chicken, and fold.
8. Add beans, salad and salsa to tacos or serve on the side.

YIELD: *Serves 4 to 6*

VARIATIONS:
  Marinate chicken in bottled Italian oil-and-vinegar dressing.
  Purchase a cooked roasted chicken from the supermarket. Cut up or shred and serve.

Poached Fish Tacos

PREPARATION TIME: *10 minutes*
COOKING TIME: *10 minutes*
TOTAL TIME: *20 minutes*

2   tablespoons lemon juice
2   tablespoons chopped fresh cilantro
1   16-ounce can chicken broth
1   pound fresh fish fillets
12 corn tortillas

CONDIMENTS:
    Lettuce or cabbage, shredded
    Cheddar and Jack cheese, shredded
    Tomatoes, finely chopped
    Sour cream
    Salsa

1. Place lemon juice, cilantro, and chicken broth in a large skillet over medium-high heat and bring to a simmer.
2. Add fish, overlapping pieces if necessary.
3. Bring broth to a boil, quickly reduce heat, cover, and simmer until fish flakes (5 to 7 minutes).
4. Drain broth from fish and set aside.
5. Soft-fry corn tortillas and keep warm.
6. Place fish chunks on tortillas and fold to form tacos.
7. Serve with condiments to be added by each creative diner.

YIELD: *Serves 6*

"At the Guadalajara market, thick, yellowish tortillas are still pressed one at a time and griddle baked."
—RICK BAYLESS AND DEANN GROEN BAYLESS
Authentic Mexican

There is documentable evidence of a dish that goes back to at least 1798 when the eggs of *moscos de pájaro* (water bugs) were gathered from "bundles of reeds stuck upright in the muck of shallow water. People 'harvest' the bundles, dry them out, and shake the eggs onto cotton sheets." In those days they were eaten in *tamales* and *tortillas*.
—RAYMOND SOKOLOV "Before the Conquest," from *Natural History* magazine

Barbecued Fish Tacos

"Three nickles will get you on the subway, but garlic will get you a seat."
—NEW YORK YIDDISH SAYING
The Garlic Lovers' Cookbook Volume II

Tex-Mex is a vague term often used as a catchall referring to the blending of Texan and Mexican cooking. Texas adopted tortillas and beans to serve with its beef barbecue and learned the Mexican skill in blending the flavors of hot peppers and spices. The Mexican stew called *carne con chile* gave rise to the "chili" served by the street vendors in San Antonio in the 1800s. Tex-Mex purists insist on making chili with shredded or cubed beef, not ground beef, and are particularly emphatic about omitting tomatoes and beans. Huevos rancheros Tex-Mex style are fried eggs and salsa ranchero over corn or wheat tortillas with perhaps a dollop of sour cream. Tex-Mex fajitas have their roots in *carne asada* and are now made from various cuts of beef as well as chicken and even fish.

PREPARATION TIME: *10 minutes*
COOKING TIME: *15 to 20 minutes*
TOTAL TIME: *1 hour*

MARINADE:

4 tablespoons (½ stick) butter or margarine, melted
1 garlic clove, minced
¼ cup lemon juice or dry white wine
½ teaspoon Worcestershire sauce
Dash of hot pepper sauce
¼ teaspoon paprika

1 pound fresh fish fillets (red snapper or other firm fish)
12 corn tortillas

GARNISHES AND CONDIMENTS:

1 medium tomato, chopped
2 cups chopped lettuce or cabbage
¼ cup sliced green onions (optional)
½ cup tomatillo salsa (page 37) or salsa picante (page 33), or bottled picante or taco sauce
1 avocado, cubed
Cilantro springs

1. Combine marinade ingredients in a 9 × 13-inch dish or plastic bag.
2. Place fish in marinade and marinate for 30 minutes at room temperature, or for 2 hours in refrigerator.
3. Drain fish, reserving marinade, and arrange on a well-greased wire grill or basket.
4. Place grill 4 to 6 inches above solid bed of low-glowing coals.
5. Cook, basting frequently with marinade, for 8 to 10 minutes on each side, or until fish flakes readily.
6. Warm tortillas briefly on grill, turning once.
7. Cut fish into serving pieces. Serve with bowls of garnishes and condiments. Have each person build his own taco.

YIELD: *Serves 4 to 6*

Potato Tacos

PREPARATION TIME: *10 minutes*
COOKING TIME: *10 minutes*
TOTAL TIME: *20 minutes*

3   tablespoons vegetable oil
1   pound red potatoes, diced (¼ inch) with skins on
1   small onion, diced
1   cup (4 ounces) shredded Cheddar cheese
½   cup red chile sauce (pages 26–29) or salsa (pages 33–37)
    Salt to taste
12 corn tortillas

CONDIMENTS:
   Lettuce, shredded
   Jalapeño peppers
   Sour cream
   Fresh tomatoes, chopped
   Bacon or ham pieces

1. Heat oil in a large skillet over medium-high heat, stir in potatoes and onion, and cook, covered, until almost tender (5–10 minutes).
2. Turn potatoes and onions and cook until tender and brown.
3. Stir in cheese, sauce, and salt.
4. Remove from heat.
5. Soft-fry tortillas (page 6).
6. Spoon potato mixture down center of tortillas and fold.
7. Serve on a platter with condiments in bowls on the side and have everyone create his own tacos.

YIELD: *Serves 4 to 6*

"Live within your harvest."
—PERSIUS
Satires

These tacos provide an amazingly simple, low-cost, tasty meal.

In Mexico, tacos are usually eaten as a snack between meals or in the evening along with a bowl of soup for supper. They are also eaten as an appetizer before the main meal of the day and are always a finger food. So, if you want to authenticate your eating experience, be like our friends south of the border: Don't eat a taco with a knife and fork!

"Eight types of tortilla and six types of tamal are consumed in Juchitán, and on a good day, you can find them all for sale by women of the market streets."
—DICK J. REAVIS
Conversations with Moctezuma

"Tacos are to Santa Fe cookery what pretzels are to beer. One can just keep on eating finely fried, crisp tortillas wrapped around a savory filling and doused with a mild to hot chili sauce, or so it seems."
—JIM DOUGLAS
Santa Fe Cookery

Beef Fajitas

PREPARATION TIME: *15 minutes*
COOKING TIME: *15 minutes*
TOTAL TIME: *4 hours or overnight*

1½   pounds skirt, flank, or round steak

MARINADE:
¼   cup olive oil
¼   cup soy sauce
½   cup tequila (optional)
3   tablespoons vinegar
2   garlic cloves, minced
½   teaspoon garlic powder
1   teaspoon dry mustard
1   teaspoon ground cumin
1   teaspoon dried oregano
½   teaspoon crushed red pepper

1   medium bell pepper, sliced in lengthwise strips
1   medium onion, sliced in lengthwise strips
12   whole green onions (eliminate for microwave or stir-fry methods)
1   medium tomato, cut into small wedges
12   9-inch flour or corn tortillas, warmed

OPTIONAL GARNISHES:
    Salsa (pages 33–37)
    Sour cream
    Guacamole (page 39)
    Cilantro

1. Trim and slice meat into thin strips.
2. Stir together the marinade ingredients
3. Place meat and marinade into a plastic bag or in a shallow glass dish.
4. Marinate in refrigerator at least 4 hours or overnight, turning three or four times.
5. Remove meat from marinade, reserving liquid.

6. Grill meat on barbecue (or under oven broiler) to desired doneness, brushing with marinade once or twice.
7. Heat skillet over medium-high heat and sauté pepper and onion in 4 tablespoons marinade for 3 to 5 minutes until crisp-tender.
8. Dip whole green onions in marinade and lightly grill or broil.
9. Add tomato to pepper and onion at last minute to warm.
10. Place a tortilla across the palm of your hand, fill with meat and sautéd vegetables, and fold. Repeat with remaining tortillas.
11. Serve with grilled or broiled green onion and choice of garnishes.

YIELD: *Serves 4 to 6*

VARIATIONS:

Use chicken, turkey, or pork tenderloin instead of beef.

Marinade can be a prepared Italian oil-and-vinegar salad dressing.

Stir-fry method:

1. Stir-fry pepper and onion in 2 tablespoons marinade until crisp-tender; remove from pan.
2. Stir-fry meat until done, 3 to 5 minutes.
3. Stir in tomato, pepper and onion and heat through.
4. Spoon into warm tortillas and fold.

Microwave method:

1. Microwave meat on high for 5 to 10 minutes until tender, stirring after 2 minutes, and set aside.
2. Microwave pepper and onion in 2 tablespoons marinade on high for 4 to 5 minutes until crisp-tender.
3. Add tomato and meat. Mix lightly and microwave on high for 1 to 2 minutes until hot.
4. Spoon into warm tortillas and fold.

Patricia Quintana, in her book, *Mexico's Feasts of Life,* describes cilantro (Chinese parsley) as easy to grow and, in appearance, like a cross between parsley and maidenhair fern. It is best when fresh, is used in many Mexican and Oriental dishes, and is now found in the produce section of most supermarkets. Use the leaves and only the tender stems. Moisture quickens its decay so keep it dry; it does not store well.

Antojitos can be literally called *little whims* and refer to foods that can be eaten out of the hand throughout the day. Many of the tortilla dishes that are thought of as main dishes in the United States are considered snack food in Mexico.

Basic Bean and Cheese Burrito

PREPARATION TIME: *10 minutes*
COOKING TIME: *0 minutes*
TOTAL TIME: *10 minutes*

2   cups refried beans (page 22), or 1 16-ounce can refried beans, heated
8   9-inch flour tortillas, warmed
1   cup (4 ounces) shredded Cheddar cheese

1. Place approximately ¼ cup beans just below center of each tortilla.
2. Sprinkle 1 to 2 tablespoons cheese over beans.
3. Fold up burrito style (page 89).
4. Serve to eat out of hand like a hot dog.

YIELD: *Serves 4 to 6*

VARIATIONS:

Microwave method: For making individual burritos, place unheated filling on unheated flat tortilla and place on a paper towel in microwave. Heat on high for 20 to 30 seconds until flexible. Fold tortilla and heat on high for another 20 to 30 seconds to heat filling thoroughly.

Fillings: Shredded beef (page 18), chicken (page 16), pork (page 20), ground beef (page 21), rice, diced potatoes, hard-boiled eggs, any leftovers.

Garnishes: Add at last minute, to prevent sogginess, or arrange on top of burrito or on plate: lettuce, chopped tomatoes, table salsas, sour cream, ripe olives, avocados.

Wet burrito: Top with red chile sauce (pages 26–29) or green chile sauce (pages 30–32) and cheese and heat in oven or microwave just to heat sauce and melt cheese.

Crisp: Fry folded burrito in a dry skillet on medium-high heat for crunchiness and toasty flavor.

Burrito grande: Use 12- to 15-inch flour tortillas and increase amount of filling.

Breakfast Burritos

PREPARATION TIME: *5 minutes*
COOKING TIME: *5 minutes*
TOTAL TIME: *10 minutes*

3 tablespoons butter
8 eggs
¼ cup canned chopped green chiles, drained
   Salt and pepper
   Dash of cayenne pepper or liquid hot pepper sauce
½ cup (2 ounces) shredded Jack or Cheddar cheese
6 9-inch flour tortillas, warmed
¼ cup salsa picante (page 33), red chile sauce (pages 26–29), or green chile sauce (pages 30–32)

1. Heat butter in a medium skillet over medium heat and scramble eggs.
2. Stir in chiles just before eggs set.
3. Remove skillet from heat. When eggs are set, add salt, pepper, and cayenne and gently stir in cheese.
4. Spoon equal amounts onto tortillas, add a teaspoon of salsa, and fold burrito style (page 89).

YIELD: *Serves 4 to 6*

VARIATIONS:

Add: fried cubed potatoes; cooked sausage or ham; chopped jalapeño peppers; avocado slices; chopped green onions.

Machaca Burrito: In a medium skillet over medium-high heat, cook ½ pound diced round steak seasoned with 1 teaspoon dry mustard and 1 teaspoon Worcestershire sauce until done. Reduce heat to medium, add 6 eggs, and scramble with ½ cup diced onion and ½ cup diced green pepper. Scoop into tortillas and fold up for a hearty breakfast to eat out of hand.

"Food goes through the eyes before it passes the mouth."
—OLD MEXICAN PROVERB

"These are often quite hot with green chile, but in truth, any of the fillings customary for burritos might be served in the morning."
—HUNTLEY DENT
The Feast of Santa Fe

"Dressed for riding the range, Yorba and Grijalva took their morning coffee and tortillas in the front courtyard, where the sun had not yet touched giant tree ferns, palms, or bamboo. There was the damp earth scent and fragrance of flowers, the song of birds. This was the best part of the day. Slowly they ate their tortillas, which had been pounded from corn raised on the rancho, sifted and made into patties neither too thick nor too thin, and baked exactly right."
—EDNA DEU PREE NELSON
The California Dons

Chimichangas

PREPARATION TIME: *10 minutes*
COOKING TIME: *15 minutes*
TOTAL TIME: *25 minutes*

2 cups ground beef filling (page 21), shredded pork (page 20), or beef filling (page 18)
6 9-inch flour tortillas
   Vegetable oil

GARNISHES:
¾ cup (3 ounces) shredded Cheddar cheese
1 cup sour cream
1 cup guacamole (page 39)
¼ cup salsa picante (page 33)

1. Spoon ⅓ cup meat filling down the center of each tortilla and fold burrito style (page 89).
2. Fry in a deep-fat fryer or 1 inch hot oil in skillet over high heat, turning until tortilla is golden—taking 1 to 2 minutes. Drain. Keep in a warm place until all tortillas are fried.
3. Serve with 2 or 3 tablespoons of each of the garnishes.

YIELD: *Serves 4*

VARIATION: Instead of deep-fat frying, set the chimichangas seam side down in a greased baking dish. Bake at 475°F until golden (7 to 10 minutes).

Toritos

PREPARATION TIME: *10 minutes*
COOKING TIME: *10 minutes*
TOTAL TIME: *20 minutes*

12 ounces Jack cheese, cut into strips: ¼ x ¼ x 4 inches
 8 9-inch flour tortillas, softened
 1 7-ounce can whole green chiles, drained
 1 cup salsa picante (page 33) or red chile sauce
    (pages 26–29)
    Vegetable oil

1. Place evenly distributed amounts of cheese on one side of each tortilla.
2. Cut chiles into strips and place on top of cheese strips.
3. Spoon 2 tablespoons of sauce over chiles and cheese.
4. Fold tortillas as for burritos (page 89).
5. Heat ¼ inch of oil in a skillet on high heat.
6. Place toritos in skillet and fry quickly, turning once, until brown and cheese is melted, or deep fry.
7. Serve whole, passing remaining sauce, or slice into appetizer-size pieces to dip.

YIELD: *Serves 4, or 16 as appetizers or snacks*

Torito means little bull in Spanish.

In *Mexico's Feast of Life*, the authors describe another kind of torito that takes on a totally different meaning in Mandinga Beach, in Veracruz. Instead of tortilla food, there it is a beverage specialty of the town, a rum drink that is prepared with any one of a dozen fruit flavors including guava, coconut, or pineapple.

"The staple diet of all true Mexicans—the bread of Mexico—is the tortilla. It is a sort of flat, round grayish pancake, made of white corn, mashed and baked on a hearth. Tortillas were made by the Aztecs, long before Hernando Cortés looked down on the walls of Tenochtitlán."
—GREEN PEYTON
San Antonio, City in the Sun

Lard is traditionally used in Mexican cuisine, but equal amounts of shortening or vegetable oil can be substituted. The flavor, however, will not be the same.

This Six-Foot Burro calls for a fiesta and a theme party! What about your own Cinco de Mayo party this year? (That's the 5th of May.)

Cinco de Mayo marks the day in 1862 when Mexico successfully rejected France's advances strategized by Napoleon. Mexico celebrates this holiday with some parades and fiestas in the larger cities but it is their true Independence Day, which celebrates the day in 1810 when Mexico proclaimed its freedom from Spain's three-hundred-year domination that is celebrated everywhere with enormous fiestas, sometimes lasting several days. It begins with the "grito"—the cry for independence—by the president on the night of September 15.

The authors of *Mexico the Beautiful Cookbook* describe the ensuing celebration on September 16: "The air reverberates with the emotional excitement of the people and the sound of exploding fireworks . . . food stalls and vendors line the streets, and restaurants are packed with people enjoying the traditional *tacos, pozole, birria,* and *enchiladas.*"

Party Time: Six-Foot Burros

PREPARATION TIME: *20 minutes*
COOKING TIME: *0 minutes*
TOTAL TIME: *20 minutes*

18 9-inch flour tortillas
3 30-ounce cans chili without beans or refried beans, heated
3 cups (12 ounces) shredded Cheddar cheese
3 cups (12 ounces) shredded Jack cheese
2 medium tomatoes, chopped
1 medium head iceberg lettuce, finely shredded
2 cups sliced green onions

GARNISHES:
1 head romaine or red lettuce
2 cups sour cream
2 cups guacamole (page 39)
½ cup chopped green onions
1 cup salsa (pages 33–37)

1. Prepare a clean board, 12 inches wide, 6 to 7 feet long.
2. Overlap tortillas down the length of the board.
3. Ladle chili down the center.
4. Sprinkle with cheeses, tomatoes, iceberg lettuce, and onions.
5. Enlisting several helpers, bring one side of the tortillas up over the filling and fold to enclose filling, tucking the seam underneath.
6. Garnish the board by placing whole lettuce leaves under the burro.
7. Cut the burro into 3-inch sections. Serve with sour cream, guacamole, green onions, and salsa.

YIELD: *Serves 20*

VARIATION: Add meat fillings (pages 16–21).

Sherried Mushroom Burritos

PREPARATION TIME: *5 minutes*
COOKING TIME: *10 minutes*
TOTAL TIME: *15 minutes*

2   tablespoons butter
1   pound fresh mushrooms, thinly sliced
1   garlic clove, minced
⅓   cup chopped green onions
¼   cup canned diced green chiles
¼   teaspoon Worcestershire sauce
4   tablespoons lemon juice
¼   cup dry sherry
½   cup sour cream
    Salt
    Pepper
6   9-inch flour tortillas, warmed

1. Melt butter in a skillet over medium-high heat and sauté mushrooms for 2 minutes.
2. Add garlic, green onions, chiles, Worcestershire sauce, and lemon juice for an additional 3 minutes.
3. Add sherry and reduce liquid to less than 1 tablespoon.
4. Add sour cream, salt, and pepper and heat to warm.
5. Spoon equal amounts of mushroom mixture onto each tortilla and fold burrito style (page 89).

YIELD: *Serves 4*

"Music I heard with you was more than music, and bread I broke with you was more than bread."
—CONRAD AIKEN
Bread and Music

"We . . . went into some of the huts, where the women were baking tortillas, one Indian custom, at least, which has descended to these days without variation. They first cook the grain in water with a little lime, and when it is soft, peel off the skin; then grind it on a large block of stone, the *metate*, or, as the Indians (who know best) call it, the *metatl*. For the purpose of grinding it, they use a sort of stone roller, with which it is crushed, and rolled into a bowl placed below the stone. They then take some of the paste, and slap it between their hands till they form it into light round cakes, which are afterwards toasted on a smooth plate, called the *comalli* (*comal* they call it in Mexico), and which ought to be eaten as hot as possible."
—FRANCES CALDERÓN DE LA BARCA
Life in Mexico, 1838

Chinese Chicken Burritos

PREPARATION TIME: *15 minutes*
COOKING TIME: *10 minutes*
TOTAL TIME: *25 minutes*

SAUCE:

¼	cup ketchup
1½	teaspoons honey
1	teaspoon Worcestershire sauce
¼	teaspoon garlic powder
2 to 3	drops of hot pepper sauce

1	pound skinless, boneless chicken breasts, cut into ½-inch cubes
2	tablespoons dry sherry
1	tablespoon teriyaki sauce
3	tablespoons vegetable oil
1	garlic clove, minced
2	slices fresh ginger
1	small dried hot red chile
½	cup chopped celery
2	green onions, thinly sliced
6 or 8	9-inch tortillas
1	cup (4 ounces) shredded Cheddar cheese

1. Stir together all sauce ingredients in a small bowl and set aside.
2. Marinate chicken in sherry and teriyaki sauce for 10 minutes.
3. Heat 2 tablespoons oil in a wok or heavy skillet over medium-high heat.
4. Add garlic, ginger, and chile and stir until chile becomes almost black.
5. Discard garlic, chile, and ginger and reduce heat to medium.
6. Add chicken and stir-fry until white in center (4 to 5 minutes). Remove and set aside.
7. Add 1 tablespoon oil to wok and stir-fry celery and green onions for 2 minutes, or until crisp-tender.

8. Add sauce and meat to wok and stir until hot. Remove from heat.
9. Spoon equal amounts of stir-fry mixture onto each tortilla, sprinkle with cheese, and fold burrito style (page 89).
10. Serve immediately.

YIELD: *Serves 4 to 6*

VARIATIONS:

Fried burritos: Rinse and wipe wok clean; heat oil over medium-high heat and brown burritos.

Substitution: Pork for chicken, increasing cooking time.

"Hot, hotter, hottest: How do we know the habañero is the hottest? By the Scoville Organoleptic Test, in use since 1912. Five heat experts taste chile pepper solutions. Three must agree before a value is assigned. Extremely hot chilies score over 10,000 units. The habañero comes in at 10,000 to 80,000. This lantern-shaped chile, about 2 inches long, looks a lot like your average sweet pepper in miniature. The resemblance stops there. It's capable of being up to eight times hotter than a jalapeño."
—*The Oregonian Foodday*
August 11, 1992

Moo Shu Burritos

"Si me he de morir, mejor
con panza llena que con
barriga vacía. If I am to
die, better with a belly
full than with belly
empty."
—MEXICAN-AMERICAN
PROVERB

In Mexico, burritos may
be called *tacos de harina*
(wheat tacos), *burritas*,
or *burros*.

"Accompanying every
norteño [northern Baja,
states of Chihuahua and
Sonora] meal is a basket
of *tortillas de harinas*
(wheat-flour tortillas), a
distinctive northern
adaptation of the corn
tortilla. Unlike the corn
version, wheat tortillas
contain fat and are
rolled rather than
flattened in a tortilla
press."
—PATRICIA QUINTANA
"A Taste of Mexico," from
Americana magazine

PREPARATION TIME:	*10 minutes*
COOKING TIME:	*10 minutes*
TOTAL TIME:	*20 minutes*

2   tablespoons vegetable oil
1   14-ounce package fresh or frozen Chinese stir-fry
     vegetables
¼   cup coarsely chopped water chestnuts
½   cup coarsely chopped bean sprouts
3   tablespoons soy sauce
6   9-inch flour tortillas, softened
¾   cup plum sauce (recipe below), or 1 7-ounce jar

1. Heat vegetable oil in a skillet or wok over medium-high
   heat until hot.
2. Place vegetables in skillet and stir-fry until crisp-tender.
3. Add water chestnuts and bean sprouts.
4. Stir in soy sauce, bring to a boil, and remove from heat.
5. Spoon ⅓ cup vegetable mixture onto tortillas, along with
   1½ tablespoons plum sauce.
6. Fold tortilla, burrito fashion (page 89).

YIELD: *Serves 4*

Note: Use your own favorite stir-fry combination or even
leftovers.

PLUM SAUCE:
6   ounces plum preserves or jelly
1   teaspoon chicken bouillon granules
2   teaspoons instant minced onions
3   tablespoons red wine vinegar
1   teaspoon soy sauce
½   teaspoon ground ginger

1. Melt preserves in a small saucepan on low heat.
2. Add remaining ingredients and bring to a boil. Reduce heat
   and simmer for 15 to 20 minutes, or until slightly thickened.

YIELD: *¾ cup*

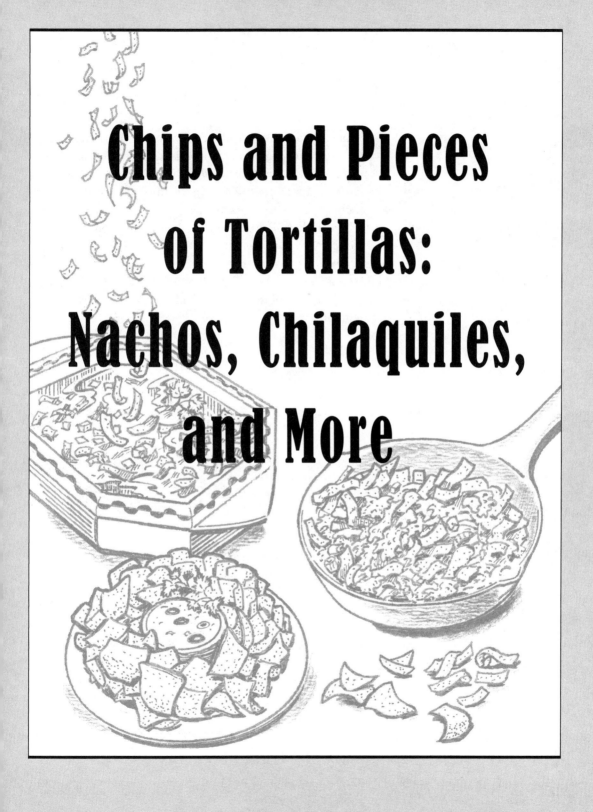

Chips and Pieces of Tortillas: Nachos, Chilaquiles, and More

What fun to think that all those unused, broken, stale pieces of tortillas can be put to good use, or that more can be done with a sack of tortilla chips than making Nachos or scooping up a great Bean Dip. Picture what could happen on a chilly day with a hearty, light or spicy Tortilla Soup, or a tortilla hash called Chilaquiles. For most gringos, that's a whole array of new taste treats. Or see what tortillas can do for a new look in a meatloaf, chicken casserole, beef stir-fry, or even a festive dessert using flour tortillas and apples. Yes, Chips and Pieces of tortillas can find themselves anywhere the imagination travels.

Nachos

PREPARATION TIME: *10 minutes*
COOKING TIME: *2 minutes*
TOTAL TIME: *12 minutes*

6   corn tortillas, cut into wedges and crisp-fried (page 6)
½   cup (2 ounces) shredded Cheddar cheese
4   fresh or canned jalapeño peppers, seeded and cut into
     thin strips

1. Arrange tortilla wedges in a single layer on ungreased baking sheet or ovenproof serving platter.
2. Sprinkle each wedge with cheese and 1 jalapeño strip.
3. Broil or microwave until cheese is melted, about 2 minutes.

YIELD: *Serves 4 to 6 as an appetizer*

VARIATION: Substitute store-bought tortilla strips or wedges for crisp-fried tortillas.

"To invite a person to your house is to take charge of his happiness as long as he is beneath your roof."
—JEAN ANTHELME BRILLAT-SAVARIN, 1759–1794
The Physiology of Taste

"Mexican food in the U.S. used to mean nachos, tacos and tamales, eaten in darkish rooms full of wrought iron, serapes, and bullfight posters. Today . . . well, for the most part, it still means nachos, tacos, and the rest. Mexican restaurants have not yet come of age hereabouts, but there's every sign that they're about to— that all the vivid colors and flavors of true Mexican cuisine will soon, at last, be brightening the American gastronomic scene."
—COLMAN ANDREWS
"Real Mexican, at Last," from *Harper's Bazaar,* 1987

"She pointed to the flushed and irritable children. See, they were all sick. They were not getting the proper food. 'What is the proper food?' Pilon demanded. 'Beans,' she said. 'There you have something to trust, something that will not go right through you.'"
—JOHN STEINBECK
Tortilla Flat

Nachos Supreme

PREPARATION TIME: *10 minutes*
COOKING TIME: *2 minutes*
TOTAL TIME: *12 minutes*

1	bag tortilla strips or chips
1	cup (4 ounces) shredded Cheddar cheese
½	cup (2 ounces) shredded Jack cheese
1	cup refried beans (page 22), or canned pinto beans or refried beans
1	medium tomato, chopped
½	cup chopped green onion
1	2¼-ounce can ripe olives, sliced
¼	cup salsa picante (page 33)
¼	cup canned diced green chiles, drained
½	cup sour cream

1. Pile tortilla strips on a large ovenproof platter and mix and toss the remaining ingredients with the chips.
2. Bake at 350°F for 10 to 12 minutes, or microwave for 2 to 3 minutes until heated through and cheese is melted.

VARIATION: Add a meat filling for a whole tortilla meal!

YIELD: *Serves 4 to 6 as an appetizer*

Nacho Bean Bake

PREPARATION TIME: *10 minutes*
COOKING TIME: *20 minutes*
TOTAL TIME: *30 minutes*

4   cups refried beans (page 22), or 1 30-ounce can refried beans
2   cups fresh or frozen corn kernels, or 1 17-ounce can whole kernel corn, drained
1   14½-ounce can stewed tomatoes, drained
1   4-ounce can chopped green chiles, drained
1   2¼-ounce can black olives, sliced
½   medium onion, finely diced
½   teaspoon chili powder
½   teaspoon garlic powder
½   teaspoon ground cumin
4   cups crushed tortilla chips
2   cups (8 ounces) shredded Cheddar cheese

1. Combine beans, corn, tomatoes, chiles, olives, onion, and spices with 2 cups crushed chips.
2. Place 1 cup crushed chips on the bottom of a 9 × 13-inch baking dish.
3. Spread bean mixture on top of chips.
4. Top with remaining crushed chips.
5. Sprinkle cheese on top.
6. Bake at 350°F for 20 minutes.

YIELD: *Serves 4 to 6*

"Beans are a warm cloak against economic cold. Only one thing could threaten the lives and happiness of the family of the Señora Teresina Cortez; that was a failure of the bean crop."
—JOHN STEINBECK
Tortilla Flat

"Corn in Mexico at the time of Cortez was so plentiful that it was often planted by the sides of the roads as a kind of free sustenance for the hungry traveler. Hunger was virtually unknown to the Aztecs of that time, thanks to maize."
—MARIA POLUSHKIN ROBBINS
American Corn

"I find, personally, one important change in taste if not in opinion. Vera Cruz cookery, which two years ago I thought detestable, now appears to me delicious! What excellent fish! And what incomparable *frijoles!*"
—FRANCES CALDERÓN DE LA BARCA
Life in Mexico, 1838

Chilaquiles

PREPARATION TIME: *10 minutes*
COOKING TIME: *10 minutes*
TOTAL TIME: *20 minutes*

8 corn tortillas
3 tablespoons oil
1 medium onion, diced
1 garlic clove, minced
1 medium tomato, chopped
1 4-ounce can diced green chiles, drained
½ cup salsa (pages 33–37)
1 cup (4 ounces) shredded Jack cheese

OPTIONAL GARNISHES:
Sour cream
Salsa
Shredded lettuce
Avocado slices
Sliced radishes
Chopped cilantro
Ripe olives

1. Stack tortillas 4 at a time and cut into 1-inch strips.
2. Heat 2 tablespoons oil in a large skillet over high heat and fry tortilla strips, a few at a time, until half crisp; drain on paper towels.
3. Add 1 tablespoon oil to skillet and sauté onion and garlic until tender and transparent.
4. Line a 9 × 13-inch ovenproof dish with a third of the tortillas. Add a third of the sautéed mixture, then a third each of the tomatoes, chiles, salsa, and cheese.
5. Repeat layers twice, making sure cheese is on top.
6. Place in a 350°F oven for 10 minutes, until cheese is melted.

YIELD: *Serves 4*

According to ancient Aztec legend, chilaquiles originally meant *broken up old sombrero*.

"After the Spanish conquered Mexico, the most noticeable shift was in their cuisine. It was a happy one that included the transformation of tortillas: after being fried or sprinkled with chorizo (a Spanish pork sausage), they turned into garnachas, chalupas, sopas, tostadas, tacos, enchiladas, chilaquiles, infladas, molotes, bocoles and pellizcadas."
—RAYMOND SOKOLOV
"How to Eat Like an Aztec," from *Natural History* magazine

VARIATIONS:

Microwave: Microwave on high until cheese melts, 3 to 4 minutes.

Skillet: Add onion and garlic to fried tortillas and cook until tender. Stir in remaining ingredients and cook gently, stirring occasionally, until tortillas are tender and cheese is melted.

Additional ingredients: 1 cup cream or sour cream; sliced or chopped ripe olives; ½ pound fried chorizo; ½ pound cooked ground beef; ½ to 1 pound cooked chicken or turkey, cubed; 1 cup refried or pinto beans; 4 to 6 eggs, slightly beaten.

Substitutions: tortilla strips or chips for tortillas; ½ cup chopped bell peppers, ¼ cup sliced pickled jalapeño peppers; or 2 fresh chopped jalapeño peppers for diced green chiles; 1 cup red or green chile sauce (pages 30–32), salsa picante (page 33), tomato sauce, or tomatillo salsa (page 37) for salsa; Cheddar or *queso fresco* for Jack cheese or a combination of cheeses; 1 cup canned tomatoes, chopped, for fresh tomatoes.

Chilaquiles include a number of thrifty yet hearty dishes with a wide range of ingredients and cooking methods and are often referred to as "dry soup" or "tortilla hash." The old, stale, and dried up pieces of tortillas take on a firm, meaty quality something like chicken, and therefore are also sometimes called "poor man's meat." This dish can be prepared in minutes and is an ideal way of dealing with those leftover dabs lurking in your refrigerator. They can be served any time of day. If you love to improvise, this is for you and it is always *chilecious*.

The custom in New Mexico is to pluck chiles from the *ristra* where they have been tied together to be dried. Sometimes they are decoratively designed into a wreath.

Bean Dip

PREPARATION TIME: *10 minutes*
COOKING TIME: *1 hour*
TOTAL TIME: *1 hour, 10 minutes*

4   cups refried beans (page 22), or 1 30-ounce can refried beans
1   8-ounce package cream cheese
1   16-ounce container sour cream
¼   teaspoon dried oregano
¼   teaspoon garlic powder
¼   teaspoon ground cumin
1   teaspoon Worcestershire sauce
1   4-ounce can diced green chiles, drained
1   cup (4 ounces) shredded Cheddar cheese
½   cup (2 ounces) shredded Jack cheese
1   large bag tortilla chips or strips

1. Mix all ingredients except Cheddar and Jack cheese and chips.
2. Place in an ovenproof casserole suitable for serving.
3. Top with cheese.
4. Bake at 250°F for 1 hour.
5. Serve with tortilla chips or strips.

YIELD: *Serves 8 to 10 as an appetizer*

NOTE: Can be used as the base for the layered dip (opposite page).

Layered Dip

PREPARATION TIME: *10 minutes*
COOKING TIME: *0 minutes*
TOTAL TIME: *10 minutes*

1 cup bean dip (opposite page), or 1 9-ounce can bean
   dip
1 cup (4 ounces) shredded Cheddar cheese
½ medium onion, chopped
1 medium tomato, chopped
1 bag tortilla chips or strips

1. Layer bean dip, cheese, onion, and tomato on a serving
   platter.
2. Surround the platter with chips for scooping.

YIELD: *Serves 4 to 6 as an appetizer*

VARIATIONS:

Layer 1 cup sour cream and ½ cup salsa over beans.

Substitutions: guacamole (page 39) for bean dip, or choose a grande fiesta platter and use bean dip as a base on one half and guacamole on the other and double the other ingredients.

Additional ingredients: green onions; ripe olives; cilantro.

"The real Mexico is one third the size of the U.S., divided into six disparate geographic regions. Each region has been tilled and shaped by a progression of keepers from the royal Aztec and Mayan Indian, through the Spanish, French, Germans, and North Americans who've called the country home. Together, they have left an aroma of toasting corn, sizzling garlic, onions, and peppers and a bit of coriander and cinnamon. In the mountains, the plains and on the gulf, Mexico's culinary eau-de-vie pursues you."
—MOLLY O'NEILL
"Mexican Jumping Scenes," from *Harper's Bazaar* magazine

Tortilla Soup with Fresh Tomato

PREPARATION TIME: *20 minutes*
COOKING TIME: *30 minutes*
TOTAL TIME: *50 minutes*

1	tablespoon butter or margarine
1	medium onion, chopped
¾	cup finely diced carrots
1	garlic clove, minced
3	14-ounce cans chicken broth
2	cups water
½	4-ounce can diced green chiles, drained
2	medium tomatoes, seeded and diced
¼	cup minced cilantro
	Salt and pepper to taste
1	tomatillo, diced (optional)
2	dashes of hot pepper sauce (optional)
3	tablespoons oil
12	corn tortillas, cut into matchstick-size strips
2	cups (8 ounces) shredded Jack cheese

1. Heat butter or margarine in a large soup pot over medium-high heat and sauté onion, carrots, and garlic until
   tender. Add remaining ingredients except oil, tortillas,
   and cheese.
2. Bring to a boil, then reduce heat, cover, and simmer for
   20 to 30 minutes.
3. Heat oil in a skillet over medium heat. Add tortilla strips
   a few at a time and fry until crisp. Drain well.
4. To serve, divide cheese and tortilla strips among six
   soup bowls. Ladle soup into bowls.
5. Pass additional cheese and tortilla strips.

YIELD: *Serves 6*

TIP: Tortilla strips can be crisped on an ungreased baking
sheet in a 400°F oven for 8 to 10 minutes. Turn several times.

Hearty Tortilla Soup

PREPARATION TIME: *20 minutes*
COOKING TIME: *20 minutes*
TOTAL TIME: *40 minutes*

1	tablespoon margarine
½	medium onion, chopped
1	garlic clove, minced
3½	cups chicken broth
1	14½-ounce can stewed tomatoes, undrained
1	8-ounce can tomato sauce
1	4-ounce can diced green chiles, drained
¼	cup minced cilantro
1	teaspoon dried oregano, crushed
2	tablespoons vegetable oil
6	corn tortillas, cut into ½-inch strips
1	cup (4 ounces) shredded Jack cheese

1. Heat margarine in a large soup pot over medium heat and sauté onion and garlic until tender.
2. Add chicken broth, undrained stewed tomatoes, tomato sauce, chiles, cilantro, and oregano.
3. Bring to a boil, reduce heat, and simmer, covered, for at least 20 minutes.
4. Heat oil in a skillet over medium heat. Add tortilla strips, a few at a time, and fry until crisp and light brown. Drain well.
5. To serve, divide cheese and tortilla strips among six soup bowls. Ladle soup into bowls and serve immediately.

YIELD: *Serves 6*

Some less obvious characteristics of *sopas* are listed in this proverb. Soup has 7 virtues: it silences hunger, provokes little thirst, makes one sleepy, also patient, always pleasant, never angry and gives flush to the face.

The basic Mexican soup is made of tomato and onion.

Cazuelas, traditional Mexican pots, are earthenware and are low-fire-glazed on the inside only. They are wide and shaped like flat-bottomed bowls. Some cooks recommend rubbing the unglazed outside with a clove of garlic to eliminate the earthy taste. Cazuelas are used for simmering stews, soups, and casseroles.

Sausage-Bean Soup

PREPARATION TIME: *10 minutes*
COOKING TIME: *2 hours*
TOTAL TIME: *3 hours*

1	pound dried pinto beans
½ to ¾	pound mild or hot Italian sausage
1	tablespoon vegetable oil
1	medium onion, diced
1	garlic clove, minced
8	cups water
1	4-ounce can diced green chiles, drained
1	teaspoon dried oregano, crushed
1	tablespoon salt
12	corn tortillas, or 2 cups crushed tortilla chips
2	cups (8 ounces) shredded Jack cheese

1. Rinse and drain beans and place in large soup pot.
2. Add water to cover beans by 2 to 3 inches.
3. Bring to a boil and cook for 2 minutes.
4. Remove pot from heat, cover, and let beans soak at least 1 hour. Drain beans, using a colander.
5. Slice sausage into ½-inch slices, brown in a skillet over medium heat and set aside.
6. Heat oil in large soup pot over medium heat and sauté onion and garlic until tender and transparent.
7. Add drained beans, water, and sausage and bring to a boil.
8. Lower heat, cover, and simmer 1½ to 2 hours, or until beans are tender.
9. About 15 minutes before soup is ready to serve, cut tortillas into ½-inch strips and place on a baking sheet. Bake at 400°F until crisp, 8 to 10 minutes, turning several times.
10. Add green chiles, oregano, and salt to soup just before serving. Ladle soup into individual bowls and top with cheese and tortilla strips or chips. Serve with extra cheese and strips.

YIELD: *Serves 6*

Huevos Rancheros Casserole

PREPARATION TIME: *10 minutes*
COOKING TIME: *20 minutes*
TOTAL TIME: *30 minutes*

3 tablespoons butter or margarine
12 corn tortillas, cut into 1-inch strips
1 14½-ounce can stewed tomatoes
1 10½-ounce can bean-with-bacon soup
1 medium onion, chopped
1 garlic clove, minced
½ cup salsa picante (page 33)
8 eggs
½ cup (2 ounces) shredded Cheddar cheese

1. Butter a 9 × 13-inch baking dish and line with tortilla pieces.
2. Drain and save juice from tomatoes.
3. Mix tomato juice with soup and pour over tortillas.
4. Heat 2 tablespoons butter in a skillet over medium-high heat and sauté onion and garlic until transparent.
5. Cut up tomatoes, add with 3 teaspoons salsa to onions, and simmer uncovered over medium heat to reduce slightly.
6. Pour tomato mixture over beans and tortillas.
7. Make 8 indentations in soup mixture with back of spoon and fill each with an egg, being careful not to break the yolk.
8. Bake at 350°F for 20 minutes, sprinkling with cheese the last 5 minutes.
9. Serve with additional salsa and hot tortillas.

YIELD: *Serves 4 to 6*

"Morning. Life within the home begins to make itself felt. The family, hurrying voices still touched with sleep, prepares to start the day. The house, little by little, becomes fragrant with the sharp odor of black coffee and the soft aroma of warm tortillas."
—PATRICIA QUINTANA WITH CAROL HARALSON
Mexico's Feasts of Life

A Mission Father to Spanish settlers in California at the turn of the eighteenth century is reported to have said, "And I brought you into a plentiful country, to eat the fruit thereof, and the goodness thereof."
—JACQUELINE HIGUERA McMAHAN
California Rancho Cooking

"Well, the fact is, a white Anglo-Saxon Protestant can't eat Eggs Ranchero in Gallup because they have a patent there on comestible liquid fire. You might as well go to Carnegie Illinois Steel and ask them to fill your pennikin at Furnace Number 2."
—RICHARD BISSELL
How Many Miles to Galena?

Layered Chicken Classic

PREPARATION TIME: *15 minutes*
COOKING TIME: *30 minutes*
TOTAL TIME: *45 minutes or overnight*

1 can cream of mushroom soup
1 can cream of chicken soup
1 cup milk or chicken broth
1 4-ounce can diced green chiles, drained
1 medium onion, chopped
1½ cups (6 ounces) shredded Cheddar cheese
1 dozen corn tortillas, torn into bits and pieces
3 cups shredded chicken filling (page 16), or 3 whole chicken breasts, cooked and shredded or cubed

1. Mix soups, milk, chiles, onion, and 1 cup cheese together in a large bowl.
2. Layer half the tortilla pieces in bottom of a 9 × 13-inch baking dish.
3. Add one layer shredded chicken on top of tortillas.
4. Pour half the soup mixture over chicken.
5. Repeat layers of tortillas, chicken, and soup mixture.
6. Refrigerate overnight (best, but not critical).
7. Bake, uncovered, for 30 minutes at 350°F.
8. Garnish with ½ cup Cheddar cheese just before serving.

YIELD: *Serves 6*

VARIATION: Microwave on high for 15 minutes.

In Mexico, there is a popular saying: "Don't make an important decision without first having eaten."
—PATRICIA QUINTANA with CAROL HARALSON
Mexico's Feasts of Life

"The festive barbecue menu hardly varied. The meat was beef or lamb. Chicken was reserved for invalids. Huge pots of thick pink beans were cooked in the same way that they had been for a hundred years. Beans were always rolled into a triangle of tortilla and they had to be thick enough so the juices did not run down your sleeve."
—JACQUELINE HIGUERA McMAHAN
"The Teens," from *Los Angeles Times Magazine*

"The deft Indian tortillera tirelessly patty-pat-patted the tortilla between chubby brown hands, stretching the elastic dough into round, flat cakes, which she baked over an open fire on a copper or iron plate, and served as fast as the feasters demanded."
—ANA BEGUÉ DE PACKMAN
Early California Hospitality

Mexican Meatloaf

PREPARATION TIME: *10 minutes*
COOKING TIME: *1 hour, 10 minutes*
TOTAL TIME: *1 hour, 20 minutes*

2   pounds lean ground beef
1   cup salsa picante (page 33) or red chile sauce (pages 26 to 29)
1   cup crushed tortilla chips
½   medium onion, chopped
1   4-ounce can diced green chiles, drained
2   eggs
1½ teaspoons salt
½   teaspoon pepper

1. Mix ground beef with ½ cup sauce and all remaining ingredients.
2. Shape into a loaf and place in a 9 × 5-inch loaf pan.
3. Bake at 350°F for 1 hour.
4. Top with remaining sauce and bake 10 minutes longer.
5. Let stand 20 minutes before slicing.

"The mere feast is nothing to the pleasure of its preparation."
—SIMMS
The Partisan, 1835

Corn tortillas, which are unleavened, are a boon to people who cannot eat foods made with yeast.

"The highlight of all celebrations was food—elaborate food which took more time to prepare, was more unusual, and often called for ingredients which had to be sent for from San Francisco."
—JACQUELINE HIGUERA McMAHAN
California Rancho Cooking

Taco Salad

PREPARATION TIME: *15 minutes*
COOKING TIME: *0 minutes*
TOTAL TIME: *15 minutes*

½   pound ground beef
1   8-ounce can kidney beans, drained and rinsed
    Salt and pepper to taste
½ to ¾   head iceburg lettuce torn into bite-size pieces
½   2¼-ounce can ripe olives, sliced
1   cup chopped green pepper
½   medium red onion, thinly sliced, or ¼cup chopped green onion
1   medium tomato, chopped
1   cup (4 ounces) shredded Cheddar cheese
1   bag plain, nacho, or taco-flavored tortilla chips
    Bottled salad dressing: thousand Island, Italian, or French
½   cup salsa picante (page 33) or bottled mild taco sauce
1   avocado, sliced
    Sour cream

1. Brown ground beef in a skillet over medium heat and drain.
2. Warm kidney beans with meat and season with salt and pepper.
3. Place lettuce in a large salad bowl and toss with olives, green pepper, onion, and tomato.
4. Add cheese and toss lightly.
5. Crush four handfuls of tortilla chips and toss with salad.
6. Pour on dressing plus 2 tablespoons salsa and toss.
7. Add meat and beans in center of salad and garnish with avocado and chips.
8. Serve with sour cream and extra salsa at the table.

YIELD: *Serves 4 to 6*
VARIATIONS:
   Substitute cooked chicken or ground beef filling (page 21) for ground beef.

Substitute seasoned meat: Brown meat with 1 cup chopped onion and add 1 8-ounce can tomato sauce, 1 tablespoon chili powder, ½ teaspoon ground cumin, ½ teaspoon dried oregano, and ¼ teaspoon salt.

Vegetarian taco salad: Omit meat.

"The bean, a native of the Americas, was easily adopted by the colonists as a food, and the Spanish-Californians paid the humble vegetable the highest tribute: 'Frijoles—frijolitos y frijoles refritos! Beans—more beans and warmed-over beans!'

"They served beans for dinner, more beans for supper, and warmed-over beans, fried dry and crisp, for breakfast. There was never a meal without frijoles in early California."
—ANA BEGUÉ DE PACKMAN
Early California Hospitality

Fractured Tacos

Served buffet style with refried beans, Mexican rice, and fresh fruit, this is an easy make-ahead meal for a crowd. Partygoers are pleased to assemble their own stacked creations and will be back for seconds.

"To Grandmama, the subject was closed. Gentle folk ate the flour tortillas that would unfold like the petals of a flower from the basket lined with a white napkin."
—JACQUELINE HIGUERA McMAHAN
California Rancho Cooking

"Traces of chiles have been found in Peruvian burial sites of 8,000 years ago. They were one of the first plants to be cultivated in the Americas. Columbus 'discovered' the chile but mistakenly thought he found the plant that produces black pepper. So he called the plant 'pepper,' a misnomer that persists today. Chiles from the Americas quickly became part of international trade. Within 100 years, they'd spread around the world."
—*The Oregonian Foodday*
August 11, 1992

PREPARATION TIME: *30 minutes*
COOKING TIME: *10 minutes*
TOTAL TIME: *30 minutes*

SPICY MEAT MIXTURE:
1   pound ground beef
½   medium onion, chopped
1   garlic clove, minced
1   7-ounce can diced green chiles, drained
1   8-ounce can tomato sauce
¼   teaspoon ground cumin
¼   teaspoon ground coriander
¼   teaspoon salt

GARNISHES AND CONDIMENTS:
½   head iceberg lettuce, chopped
1   cup (4 ounces) shredded Cheddar cheese
2   medium tomatoes, chopped
½   medium onion, chopped
1   cup salsa picante (page 33)
1   2¼-ounce can ripe olives, drained and chopped
1   cup sour cream
1   avocado, sliced, or 1 cup guacamole (page 39)
½   cup chopped cilantro
1   large bag tortilla chips or strips

1. Brown ground beef in skillet.
2. Pour off excess drippings, add onion and garlic, and cook over medium-high heat until tender and transparent.
3. Stir in remaining meat mixture ingredients and simmer for 10 minutes.
4. Serve each portion beginning with a layer of tortilla chips topped with meat mixture, and then let diners add all or any of the garnishes and condiments.

YIELD: *Serves 4 to 6*

Beef Stir-Fry

PREPARATION TIME: *15 minutes*
COOKING TIME: *15 minutes*
TOTAL TIME: *30 minutes*

½ head romaine lettuce
1 to 1½ pounds top round steak, partially frozen
2 tablespoons vegetable oil
1½ teaspoons ground cumin
1½ teaspoons dried oregano
1 garlic clove, minced
½ green bell pepper, seeded and cut into strips
½ red bell pepper, seeded and cut into strips
1 large onion, cut into thin strips
2 fresh jalapeño peppers, seeded, deveined, and cut into thin strips
4 cups packaged tortilla chips or strips

1. Stack lettuce leaves with largest on bottom, then roll up starting at long edge, and cut crosswise into thin strips.
2. Make a bed of lettuce strips on a large serving platter.
3. Slice beef across grain into ⅛-inch-thick strips
4. Combine oil, cumin, oregano, and garlic in a bowl.
5. Heat half the seasoned oil in a large skillet or wok over medium heat.
6. Add beef, a few slices at a time, and stir-fry for 2 to 3 minutes.
7. Remove beef and set aside.
8. Add remaining seasoned oil to skillet and stir-fry vegetables until crisp-tender, 2 to 3 minutes.
9. Return meat to skillet and stir-fry until heated.
10. Add tortilla chips to skillet and quickly toss.
11. Mound mixture in center of lettuce bed and garnish with chips around edge.

YIELD: *Serves 4 to 6*

"The honest flavor of fresh garlic is something I can never have enough of."
—JAMES BEARD
Beard on Food

"Spaniards introduced methods of cookery. Meat was thinly sliced in long sheets and then sprinkled with salt and herbs and smoked for storage, leading to the habit of cutting meat with the grain."
—GEORGE C. BOOTH
The Food & Drink of Mexico

From the diary of sixteenth-century Franciscan friar Bernardino de Sahagún, *General History of the Things of New Spain*, we know that the Aztecs' diet was based on corn and tortillas, tamales and plenty of chiles in many varieties. His research provides evidence for a continuity between Aztec food and popular Mexican food of today.

Fried Mexican Ice Cream

PREPARATION TIME: *15 minutes*
COOKING TIME: *10 minutes*
TOTAL TIME: *2 to 3 hours*

½	gallon vanilla ice cream
6	8-inch flour tortillas
2	teaspoons cinnamon
4	teaspoons sugar
2	eggs
	Oil for deep-frying
	Honey
½	pint heavy cream, whipped

1. Scoop ice cream into 7 balls (this allows 1 extra, just in case there is a mistake made in the frying, to save you from having to start the process over.)
2. Freeze ice cream balls.
3. Place tortillas on rack in oven and bake at 450°F until dry and crisp but not brown.
4. Crush tortillas with a rolling pin into fine crumbs, or crumble them in a plastic bag.
5. Mix crumbled tortillas, cinnamon, and sugar in a shallow bowl.
6. Roll frozen ice cream balls in the crumb mixture.
7. Refreeze ice cream balls.
8. Beat eggs and dip coated balls in egg and roll again in the crumbs.
9. Repeat egg and crumb coating several times until the crumbs are all used up. Don't omit this egg dipping; the egg acts as glue.
10. Return balls to the freezer until ready to use.
11. Heat oil to 350°F in a deep-fat cooker or at least a 5-inch-deep pan to prevent oil from spilling over.
12. Place 1 ice cream ball at a time in hot oil for 1 minute. Immediately remove to a chilled dessert dish.

13. Top ice cream with a drizzle of honey and a generous tablespoon of whipped cream.
14. Serve immediately. The balls will be crunchy on the outside and just beginning to melt on the inside.

YIELD: *Serves 6*

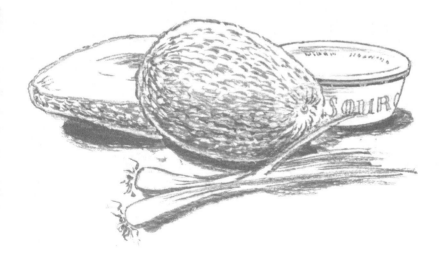

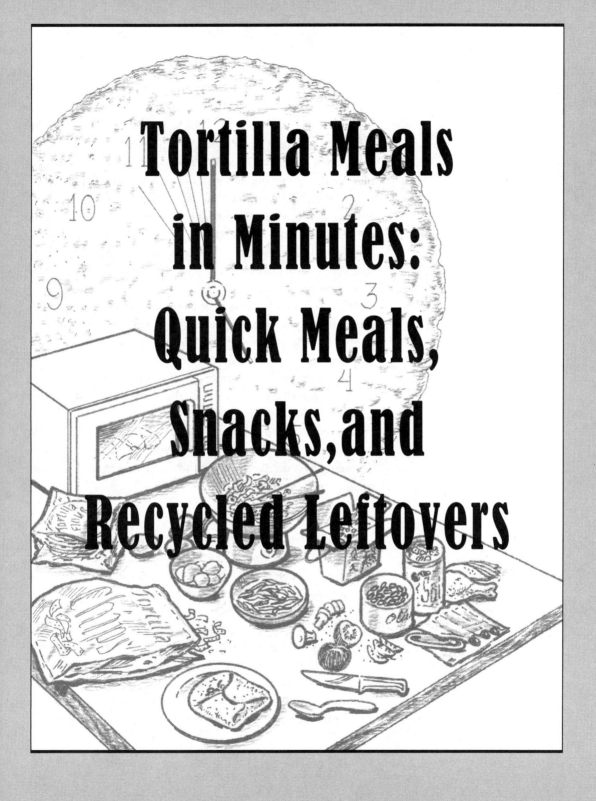

Tortilla Meals in Minutes:
Quick Meals, Snacks, and Recycled Leftovers

You've arrived home late. You're tired and hungry and the kids are nutty. You open the refrigerator door, then the cupboards. It looks hopeless. There are just bits and pieces of food. Before you give in to the urge to pile everyone into the car and head for Taco Bell, stop! Take courage. Try looking at your situation through the eye of a tortilla. All those leftovers and odds and ends are *ingredients* to fill a tortilla. With a little imagination, they become the makings for tostados, tacos, quesadillas, burritos, enchiladas, taquitos, nachos, and chilaquiles.

Below is a list of at least some of those items you may have found when you opened the doors to your refrigerator and cupboards. Here's your chance to turn them into fun tortilla fixings and orchestrate a quick home meal instead of spending a small fortune on commercial fast food. Some of these ideas—especially the roll-ups—make ideal portable snacks for tortilla lovers on the run.

Re-energize with a burst of hope. Here you have a whole new look for leftovers: a face-lift. Within minutes, dinner is on the way as the spirit of the tortilla strikes again! Let your imagination run *poco loco!*

PEANUT BUTTER

- Spread peanut butter on a warmed flour tortilla; top with bananas, raisins, shredded carrots, chopped apple, chopped celery, cream cheese, or even jelly. Roll it up for a nutritious lunch or on-the-run snack.

CHEESE

- Shred cheese and build a quesadilla (page 72), adding green onion, olives, tomatoes, celery, green or red peppers, beans, chiles, chicken, salsa, or sour cream. If all you have are tortilla chips or strips, use the cheese to make an impromptu, unfancy plate of nachos (page 111).

- Leftover chicken or beef is the basis for a burrito (page 89). Just keep stuffing the cheese, rice, beans, potatoes, and taco sauce or salsa, along with the meat, into one of those tortillas you found.

- Make a set of enchiladas (pages 42–45) by chopping up that leftover meat and adding the cheese, onions, olives, and enchilada sauce or tomato sauce spiked with the taco sauce. Heat in the microwave until the cheese starts oozing.

- If you're feeling energetic, you could turn your rolled-up enchilada into a taquito (page 63) by rolling it tightly, deep-frying it, and adding a topping of leftover sour cream.

- Leftover chicken or turkey can be stir-fried along with carrots, bean sprouts, bok choy, water chestnuts, and sliced onions. Spoon the mixture into a warmed flour tortilla, sprinkle some teriyaki sauce and/or Jack cheese over the top, and roll it up. You're on your way!

- Leftover ground beef can be made into hamburger patties. While the burgers are frying, warm three tortillas per person. Fold them into quarters and place three on each plate to form a circle. Put the burger on top, adding jalapeños, cheese, tomatoes, lettuce, and other hamburger fixin's.

- For a Mexican chili dog, roll up a hot dog inside a flour tortilla, smother it with chili and cheese, and zap it in the microwave until steaming.

- Roll up a hot dog inside a corn or flour tortilla. Quick-fry or microwave and dip in salsa before each tasty bite. Add salsa, mayonnaise, or salad dressing along with lettuce and tomato for a Mexican hot dog.

- Layer five six-inch flour tortillas with thinly sliced deli meats such as ham or turkey and cheese. Place on a paper plate and cover with a paper towel. Microwave until heated through and cheese is melted. Cut into pie-shaped slices.

TUNA

- Add celery, lettuce, tomato, onions, pickle, and mayonnaise. Roll up in a flour tortilla.
- Serve tuna on a bed of corn chips for tuna salad nachos.

COOKED VEGETABLES

- Combine cooked veggies with cooked rice, salsa, meat, potato, or cheese in a burrito (page 89) and top with sour cream and/or guacamole (page 39).

SALAD FIXIN'S

- Create a tostada (page 70) by stacking a crisp tortilla base with beans, meat, lettuce, tomato, cucumber, sprouts, green onion, peppers, or cheese.
- Make a taco salad by tossing leftover salad with chips and salsa.
- Use leftover salad to create a burrito grande (page 100).

COOKED RICE

- Stuff a burrito (page 89) with rice, beans, meat, cooked veggies, or leftover Chinese stir-fry. Zap it in the microwave before serving.

BEANS: CHILI, REFRIED, PINTO, OR KIDNEY

- Add beans (along with odds and ends of cheese, salsa, tomato, and onion) to a taco salad or nachos, chilaquiles, tostadas, or tacos.
- Spread beans on a corn tortilla, sprinkle with onion and cheese, and pop in the toaster oven or under the broiler.
- Stuff a burrito (page 89) with beans and almost anything else in the refrigerator.
- Make a Chili Billy: chips topped with chili and cheese and heated.

POTATOES

- Cube cooked potatoes and fry them with onion and chiles, meat, cheese, or eggs for burritos (page 89) or tacos (page 88).

TACO SAUCE OR SALSA

- Use taco sauce or salsa to spice up almost any leftover dish you may find in the refrigerator. Add chips or tortillas for a quick-and-easy meal.
- Spike leftover salad dressing with taco sauce or salsa and mix with meat and cheese for a burrito (page 89) or a taco salad (page 124).

SOUR CREAM

- A little sour cream makes a sublime topping for any kind of burrito, tostada, taco, taco salad, or enchilada.

BUTTER

- For a quick snack, spread a warm tortilla with butter and sprinkle with garlic salt *or* powdered chili *or* cinnamon-sugar *or* drizzle with honey and sprinkle with cinnamon. For crisp tortillas, place them on a paper towel and pop in the microwave for 1 minute or less and sprinkle with goodies.

CHINESE FOOD

- Reheat leftover Chinese food and add soy, teriyaki, or plum sauce. Fold mixture into a burrito (page 89) and deep-fry for a Chinese chimichanga or a Mexican egg roll.

EGGS

- Poach or fry eggs for huevos rancheros (page 78) or for topping enchiladas.
- To create an eggy filling for burritos or tacos, combine leftover cooked potatoes and/or lunch meat, chiles, onion, and bell pepper, then add beaten eggs and cook in a skillet over medium-high heat until set. This Mexican omelet can also be tossed with taco chips.

SALAD DRESSING

- Mix salad dressing with meat and cheese, spike with taco sauce, and use as a filling for burritos (page 89) or for a taco salad (page 124).

May you have a tortilla in your hand,
Warmth around your table,
Peace in your heart, and
Joy along the way.

Pat and Barbara

Spanish Pronunciation Guide and Glossary

Burrito (boo-RREE-toh): a folded tortilla wrapped around a hot filling—usually refried beans and cheese

Chilaquiles (chee-lah-KEE-less): a casserole dish that can use stale pieces of tortillas and a variety of garnishes

Chile (CHEE-lay): any of a variety of peppers, usually referring to the long green variety

Chile Verde (CHEE-lay BEHR-theh): a green chile sauce used as a garnish or the basis for a type of sauce

Chimichanga (chee-mee-CHAN-gah): a deep-fried crisp burrito, literally a thingamajig

Chorizo (choh-REE-soh): spicy pork sausage

Cilantro (see-LANH-troh): fresh leaves of coriander used in cooking and as a garnish

Enchilada (ehn-chee-LAH-thah): a tortilla dipped in a sauce and filled with cheese and a variety of other ingredients

Epazote (eh-pah-SOH-teh): herb commonly used in Mexican cooking

Fajitas (fa-HEE-tas): spiced, shredded meat and vegetables spooned into a soft, warmed tortilla

Flautas (FLOU-tas): a tortilla filled typically with chicken, rolled to resemble a flute, and fried crisp

Frijoles Refritos (free-HOH-less rreh-FREEH-tohs): refried beans, usually pinto beans

Guacamole (gwah-kah-MOH-ley): a thick sauce made of avocados

Huevos Rancheros (WEH-vohs rran-CHAY-rohs): poached or fried eggs served on a fried tortilla and garnished with a sauce

Jalapeño (hah-lah-PEH-nyoh): a small, fat, green, and relatively hot chile pepper used fresh or canned

Maíz (mah-EES): dried corn

Masa (MAH-sah): a dough made of ground, dried corn and water used to make tortillas

Masa Harina (MAH-sah ah-REE-nah): corn flour used to make masa dough

Metate (meh-TAH-teh): a flat, rectangular tripod of stone used for grinding corn and chiles

Molcajete (mohl-kah-HEH-teh): mortar for grinding chiles and sauces

Nachos (NAH-chos): tortilla chips smothered in melted cheese and other garnishes and sauces

Picadillo (pee-kah-DEE-yoh): a mixture of meats and other ingredients, including spices such as cinnamon and raisins, used as a filling for tortillas

Quesadilla (keh-sah-DEE-yah): a tortilla that is served either flat and covered with melted cheese and other ingredients, or folded and crisped

Queso (KEH-soh): cheese

Salsa Fresca (SAHL-sah FREHS-kah): sauce made from fresh ingredients, including tomatoes, onions, and chiles

Salsa Picante (SAHL-sah pee-CAHN-teh): hot, spicy sauce (not hot temperature)

Sopa (SOH-pah): soup

Taco (TAH-koh): name given to a fried tortilla when it is wrapped around a filling

Taquitos (tah-KEE-tohs): a corn tortilla typically filled with chicken or beef, tightly rolled, then fried—a little rolled taco

Tomatillo (toh-mah-TEE-yoh): tart, lemon-size, light-green fruit with a papery husk; commonly used in green sauces

Topopo (toh-POH-poh): a hearty chef's salad that is commonly found along the Arizona-Mexico border (ensalada de topopo) and presented in the shape of a volcano

Torito (toh-REE-toh): a folded flour tortilla filled with chile, cheese, and a red sauce, then deep-fried

Tortilla (tor-TEE-yah): thin, unleavened pancake of ground, dried corn or wheat flour

Tostada (tohs-TAH-thah): a flat, crisply fried tortilla heaped with a variety of ingredients

Additional Resources of Special Interest to the Cook

Several cookbook authors deserve our special recognition for having contributed to our understanding of the tortilla and its place within many varied cultures and cuisines. We rest in reverence of their work, knowing that our more whimsical selection of recipes, focusing on the tortilla, would not be here had they not gone before us as a standard and inspiration.

We encourage you to read our bibliography, which lists many impressive writings, and to sample at least one of the cookbooks for a deeper appreciation of the various cuisines that include tortilla cookery: old Mexico, Southwestern, California rancho, Spanish, native Indian, Tex-Mex, and Santa Fe.

We thank Rick and Deann Groen Bayless for their research and for sharing their wanderings, introducing us to the breadth of Mexico's cooks, kitchens, markets, and feasts in their book *Authentic Mexican*.

Colorful, sunny tastes and deep, rich earthy flavors of American Southwest cooking, culture, and history, were found in Huntley Dent's *The Feast of Santa Fe*. His book provides the ingredients for many lively feasts.

Diana Kennedy remains the authority on Mexican cooking and wrote the classic book, *The Cuisines of Mexico*. In another of her books, *The Tortilla Book*, she perfectly describes the spirit of the tortilla: "Eating tortillas for the first time, you may wonder what the fuss is all about—in other words, they may leave you cold. Then one day you will begin to crave one; unconsciously they will have become a passion, an addiction for life." She also wrote *Recipes From the Regional Cooks of Mexico*.

In Jacqueline Higuera McMahan's *California Rancho Cooking*, we experience a slice of California history, along with a style of cooking that has tastes from the Indians, Spanish, Mexicans, and Latin Americans who established the ranchos and missions. Jacqueline's love of the celebration and ceremony of eating are warmly expressed in her words and recipes. She also contributed many basic treasures in *The Salsa Book*.

• • •

Bayless, Rick, and Deann Groen Bayless. *Authentic Mexican.* New York: William Morrow and Co., 1987.

Booth, George C. *The Food & Drink of Mexico.* Los Angeles: Ward Ritchie Press, 1964.

Butel, Jane. *Tex-Mex Cookbook.* New York: Harmony Books, 1980.

de la Rosa, Angeles, and C. Gandia de Fernandez. *Flavors of Mexico.* San Francisco: 101 Productions, 1987.

Dent, Huntley. *The Feast of Santa Fe.* New York: Simon and Schuster, 1985.

Douglas, Jim. *Santa Fe Cookery.* New York: Dial Press, 1978.

Jones, Evan, ed. *A Food Lover's Companion.* New York: Harper & Row, 1979.

Kennedy, Diana. *The Cuisines of Mexico.* New York: Harper & Row, 1972, revised 1986.

———. *Recipes From the Regional Cooks of Mexico.* New York: Harper & Row, 1978.

———. *The Tortilla Book.* New York: Harper & Row, 1975.

McMahan, Jacqueline Higuera. *California Rancho Cooking.* Lake Hughes, Cal.: The Olive Press, 1988.

———. *The Salsa Book.* Lake Hughes, Cal.: The Olive Press, 1986.

Sunset Mexican Cookbook. Menlo Park, Cal.: Lane Publishing, 1969.

Zelayeta, Elena. *Secrets of Mexican Cooking.* Englewood Cliffs, N.J.: Prentice Hall, 1958.

Bibliography
Works Cited in the Text

BOOKS

Anderson, Arthur J.O., and Charles E. Dibble, translated from the Nahuatl (Aztec). *The War of Conquest*. Salt Lake City: University of Utah Press, 1978.

Atlas, Nava. *American Harvest*. New York: Fawcett Columbine, 1987.

Bartlett, John. *Familiar Quotations*. Edited by Emily Morrison Beck. Boston: Little, Brown & Co., 1980.

Bayless, Rick, and Deann Groen Bayless. *Authentic Mexican*. New York: William Morrow and Co., 1987.

Beard, James. *Beard on Food*. New York: Alfred A. Knopf, 1974.

Bissell, Richard. *How Many Miles to Galena?* Boston: Little, Brown & Co., 1968.

Booth, George C. *The Food & Drink of Mexico*. Los Angeles: Ward Ritchie Press, 1964.

Brillat-Savarin, Jean Anthelme, *The Physiology of Taste*. Translated by M. F. K. Fisher. San Francisco: North Point Press, 1986.

Bullock, W. *Six Months Residence and Travels in Mexico*. London: John Murray, 1825.

Butel, Jane. *Tex-Mex Cookbook*. New York: Harmony Books, 1980.

Calderón de la Barca, Frances. *Life in Mexico, 1838*. Edited and annotated by Howard T. Fisher and Marion Hall Fisher. New York: Doubleday, 1966.

Coyle, L. Patrick Jr. *The World Encyclopedia of Food*. New York: Facts on File, 1982.

Crosby, Alfred W. *The Columbian Exchange: Biological and Cultural Consequences of 1492*. Westport, Conn.: Greenwood Press, 1972.

Dent, Huntley. *The Feast of Santa Fe*. New York: Simon and Schuster, 1985.

DeWitt, Dave, and Nancy Gerlach. *Just North of the Border*. Albuquerque: Out West Publishing, 1990.

——. *The Whole Chile Pepper Book*. Toronto: Little, Brown & Co., 1990.

Díaz del Castillo, Bernal. *The Discovery and Conquest of Mexico, 1517–1521*. Translated by A. P. Maudslay. Mexico City: Ediciones Tolteca, 1953, and New York: Farrar, Straus and Cudahy, 1956.

Dietary Guidelines for Americans, U.S. Department of Agriculture, U.S. Department of Health and Human Services, Third Edition, Home and Garden Bulletin No. 232., 1990.

Douglas, Jim. *Santa Fe Cookery*. New York: Dial Press, 1978.

Esar, Evan. *20,000 Quips and Quotes*. Garden City, N.Y.: Doubleday, 1968.

Emerson, Ralph Waldo. *Emerson: A Modern Anthology*. Ed. by Alfred Kazin and Daniel Aaron. Boston: Houghton Mifflin, 1959.

Fisher, M.F.K. *Here Let Us Feast*. New York: The Viking Press, 1946.

Flesch, Rudolf, ed. *The New Book of Unusual Quotations*. New York: Harper & Row, 1957.

The Florentine Codex, Book VI, page 239. Salt Lake City, Utah, and Santa Fe, New Mexico: University of Utah Press and The School of American Research, respectively, 1950–1982.

The Gilroy Garlic Festival Association, Inc. *The Garlic Lovers' Cookbook Volume II*. Berkeley: Celestial Arts, 1985.

Glazer, Mark, comp. *A Dictionary of Mexican American Proverbs*. New York: Greenwood Press, 1987.

Guterman, Norbert, comp. *A Book of French Quotations*. New York: Doubleday, 1963

Hardy, Thomas. *Jude the Obscure*. New York: Harper & Brothers, 1896.

Heywood, John. *Proverbs Part 2*, Fielding Covenant Garden Tragedy, 1546.

Holy Bible. (Set forth in 1611 and commonly known as the King James Version). New York: American Bible Society, 1982.

Hooker, Alan. *Vegetarian Gourmet Cookery*. Berkeley: 101 Productions, 1970, revised 1982.

Jones, Evan, ed. *A Food Lover's Companion*. New York: Harper & Row, 1979.

Juvenal and Persius. *Satires. Sat. VI*. Translated by G. G. Ramsey. London: Harvard University Press, 1918.

Lewis, Edna. *The Taste of Country Cooking.* New York: Alfred A. Knopf, 1976.

Life Application Bible—The Living Bible. Wheaton, Ill.: Tyndale House Publishers, 1988.

Kennedy, Diana. *The Cuisines of Mexico.* New York: Harper & Row, 1972, revised 1986.

McMahan, Jacqueline Higuera. *California Rancho Cooking.* Lake Hughes, Cal.: The Olive Press, 1988.

―――. *The Salsa Book.* Lake Hughes, Cal.: The Olive Press, 1986.

Nelson, Edna Deu Pree. *The California Dons.* New York: Appleton-Century-Crofts, 1962.

Nichols, John. *The Milagro Beanfield War.* New York: Holt, Rinehart, and Winston, 1974.

Olney, Richard. *Simple French Food.* New York: Atheneum, 1974.

Oxenham, John. *The Fiery Cross.* New York: George H. Doran Company, 1918.

Oxford Dictionary of Quotations, The. New York: Oxford University Press, 1941.

Packman, Ana Begué de. *Early California Hospitality.* Fresno, Cal.: Academy Library Guild, 1953.

Palazuelos, Susanna, and Marilyn Tansend. *Mexico the Beautiful Cookbook.* San Francisco: Collins Publishers, 1991.

Pepys, Samuel. *The Diary of Samuel Pepys.* London: J. M. Dent & Sons Ltd., 1906.

Peyton, Green. *San Antonio, City in the Sun.* New York: McGraw-Hill Book Co., 1946.

Quintana, Patricia, with Carol Haralson. *Mexico's Feasts of Life.* Tulsa, Okla: Council Oak Books, 1989.

Rawlins, Pat. *Women for Columbia Cookbook.* Portland: Women for Columbia Press, 1974.

Reavis, Dick J. *Conversations with Moctezuma.* New York: William Morrow and Co., 1990.

Ricardo, Don. *Early California and Mexico Cook Book.* Toluca Lake, Cal.: Pacifica House, 1968.

Robbins, Maria Polushkin. *American Corn.* New York: St. Martin's Press, 1989.

Sahagún, Fray Bernardino de. *General History of the Things of New Spain.* Translated and annotated by Arthur J. O. Anderson and Charles E. Dibble. Santa Fe, and Salt Lake

City: The School of American Research and the University of Utah Press, respectively, 1950–1982.

Scofield, C. I., ed. *Oxford NIV Scofield Study Bible, New International Version*. New York: Oxford University Press, 1984.

Steinbeck, John. *Tortilla Flat*. New York: The Modern Library, 1937.

Stevenson, Burton Egbert, ed. *Poems of American History*. Cambridge: Houghton Mifflin Co., 1908.

———, selected and arranged by. *The Home Book of Quotations*. New York: Dodd Mead & Co., 1967.

Sunset Mexican Cookbook. Menlo Park, Cal.: Lane Publishing, 1969.

Tannahill, Reay. *Food in History*. New York: Crown Publishers, 1988.

Tolbert, Frank X. *A Bowl of Red*. New York: Doubleday, 1972.

U.S. Department of Agriculture and U.S. Department of Health and Human Services. *Dietary Guidelines for Americans*. Third Edition, 1990. Home and Garden Bulletin No. 232.

U.S. Department of Agriculture, *Nutritive Value of Foods*, Human Nutrition Information Service, Home and Garden Bulletin No. 72.

Zelayeta, Elena. *Secrets of Mexican Cooking*. Englewood Cliffs, N.J.: Prentice Hall, 1958.

MAGAZINES AND NEWSPAPERS

"A Cinco de Mayo Dinner," *Gourmet*, May 1989, pp. 126–32 + .

Andrews, Colman, "Real Mexican, At Last," *Harper's Bazaar*, February 1987, p. 108 + .

Durbin, Barbara, and Naomi Kaufman Price, "Torching the Tongue," *The Oregonian Foodday*, August 11, 1992.

McMahan, Jacqueline Higuera. *Los Angeles Times Magazine*, November 4, 1990.

O'Neill, Molly. "Mexican Jumping Scenes," *Harper's Bazaar*, February 1987, p. 108 + .

Quintana, Patricia, "A Taste of Mexico," *Americana*, May/June 1987, pp. 56–59.

Robbins, Maria Polushkin, "American Corn," *Adweek*, November 7, 1988.

Sides, Susan, "The Mexican Garden Cafe," *The Mother Earth News*, May, June 1990, p. 88.

Sokolov, Raymond, "Before the Conquest," *Natural History,* August 1989, pp. 76–79.

———, "Insects, Worms and Other Tidbits," *Natural History,* September 1989, p. 84 + .

———, "How to Eat Like an Aztec," *Natural History,* November 1989, p. 110 + .

Williams, A. R., "A Different Mexican Cuisine," *Américas,* May–June 1986, p. 54.

Index